AF327744

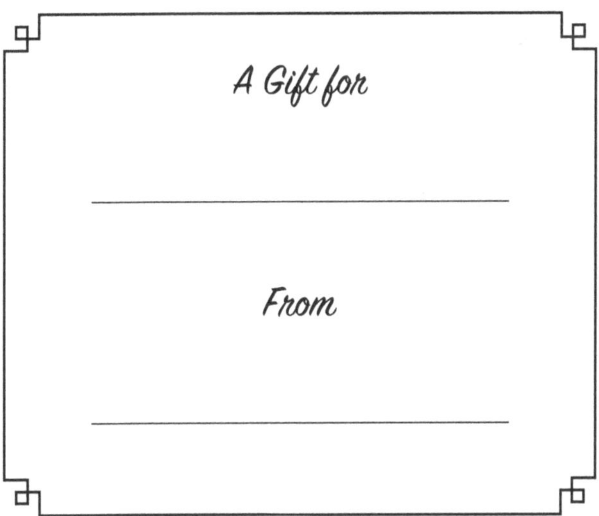

A Gift for
From

ST. AUGUSTINE

UNIQUE PLACES...
DISAPPEARING SPACES

Watercolor Paintings
by
NANCY MACRI

ST. AUGUSTINE

Unique Places...
Disappearing Spaces

Watercolor Paintings
by Nancy Macri

ISBN: 978-0-9759533-6-5

Published by
Legacies & Memories
St. Augustine, Florida
(888) 862-2754
www.LegaciesandMemoriesPublishing.com

A Legacies & Memories Book

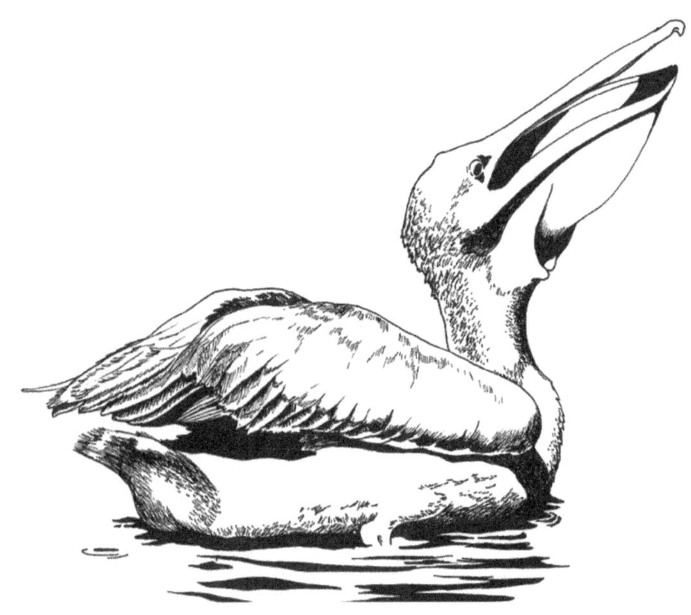

Contents

Preface

Beauty often lies in the immediately apparent, but in quiet observation can become even more clear. So it is with St. Augustine, Florida, a special and enchanting place steeped in history and verdant landscape. But many of its natural vistas are shrinking as a result of development, and far too many buildings and structures are being allowed to deteriorate despite considerable efforts at historic preservation.

In my original watercolor paintings and drawings, reproduced in this book, I felt compelled to capture certain settings and structures that caught my eye — places and spaces that seemed to speak of time's passage on many different levels. The paintings also are meant to express the connection and love I feel for the place I have called home since 1979.

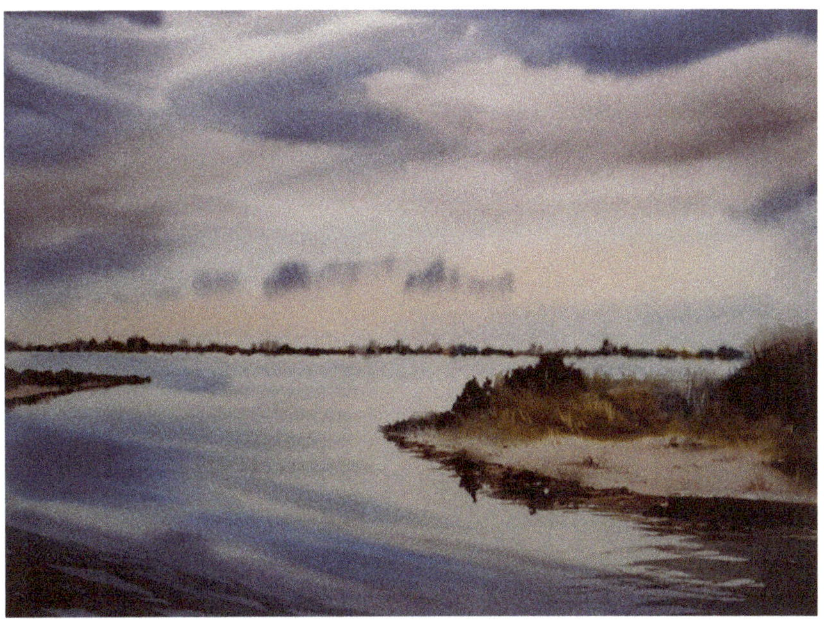

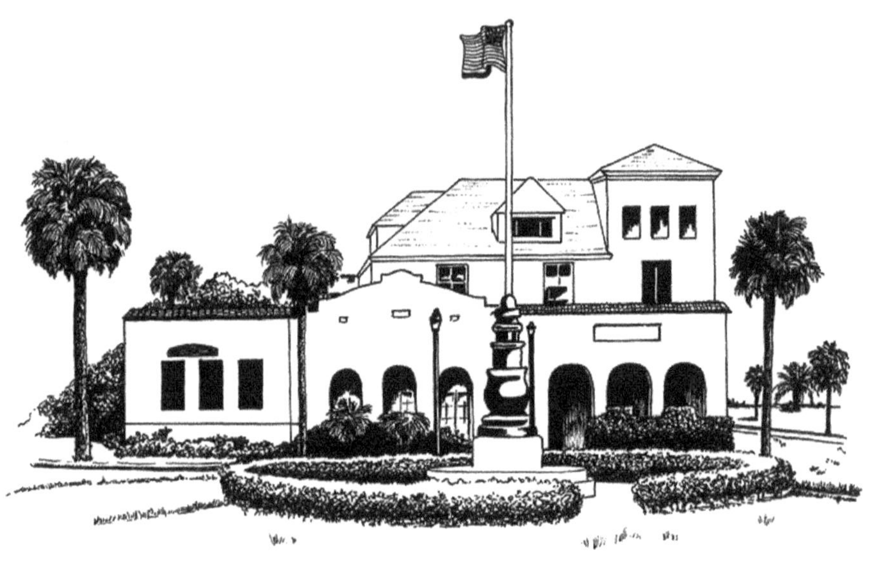

My hope is that in presenting my work it will foster a deeper love, respect, and appreciation for a place that remains unique despite centuries of change, both natural and man-made. As we observe the beauty of St. Augustine and its surrounding areas, I encourage us to pause, to take in that beauty even when it may not be readily apparent — and to focus on care and preservation.

The original watercolor paintings featured in this book were completed during the span of 2001–2003 when I became aware of St. Augustine's shrinking landscape. After the tragic events of 9/11, I began expressing that awareness though painting.

In the following pages, the paintings are presented according to location, beginning in the area of St. Augustine South, winding along US 1, north to State Road 16, then farther north to Vilano Beach along A1A. We then turn back south, returning on our journey through St. Augustine, to the downtown historic area. We travel past the Mission Nombre de Dios, the Castillo de San Marcos, meandering downtown, wandering around the grounds of what has been known as the Dow Museum of historic houses. We then take off for the southern beaches, via Anastasia Island, and drift along A1A to Summer Haven. We double back and end at a place that no longer exists, Cooksey's Campground, where there once was an oasis of tranquility and wildlife prior to development.

If one is looking for historic facts, not too many will be found here. There are enough books written about all that, in my estimation, covering St. Augustine's history in vast detail. My aim in showcasing a collection of paintings and drawings in this book is to inspire the desire to appreciate and save St. Augustine's remaining natural vistas.

Nancy Macri

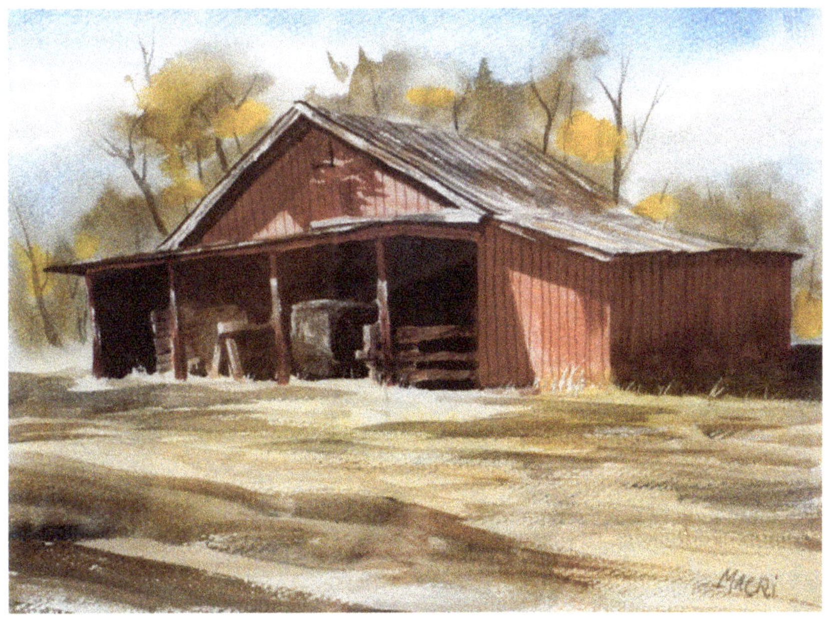

St. Augustine South

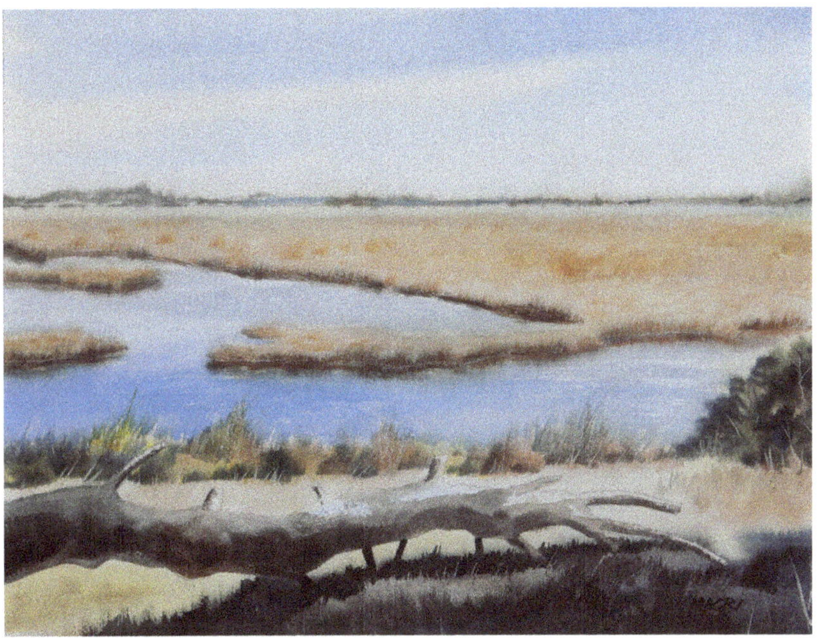

"Looking Across the Intracoastal Waterway"

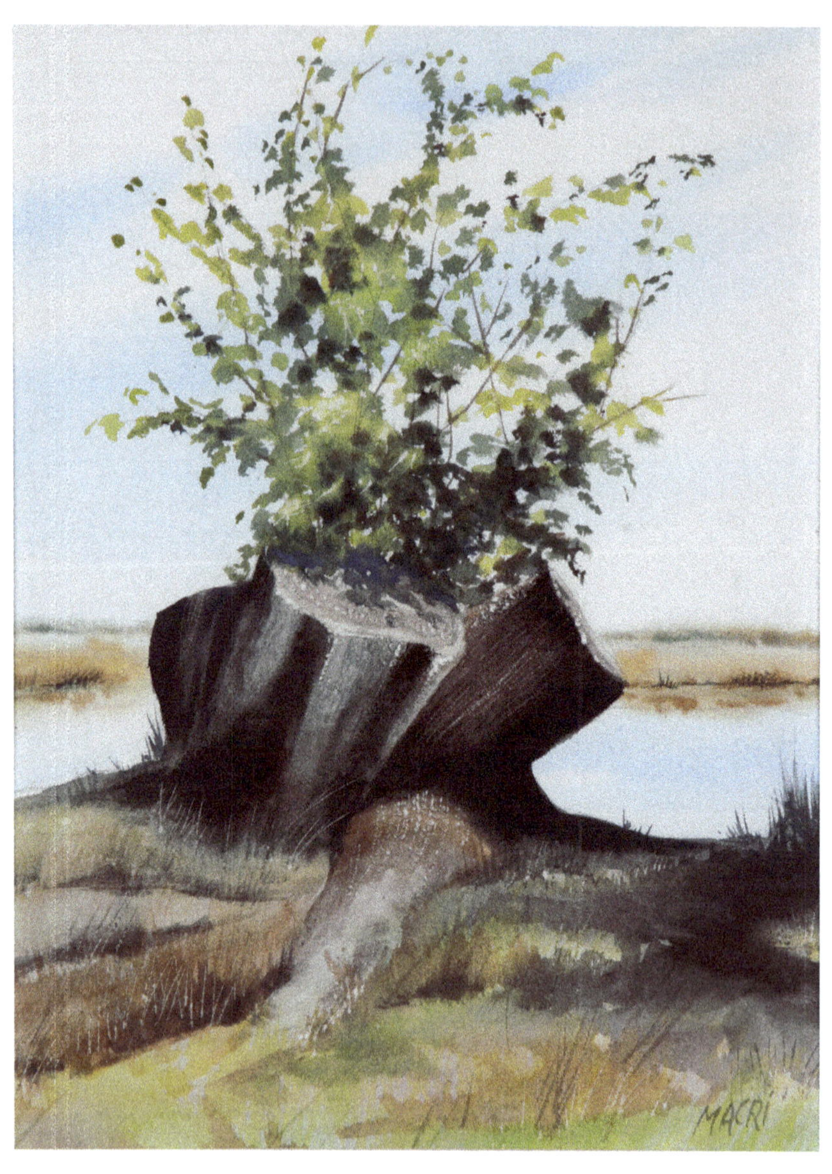

"New Life"

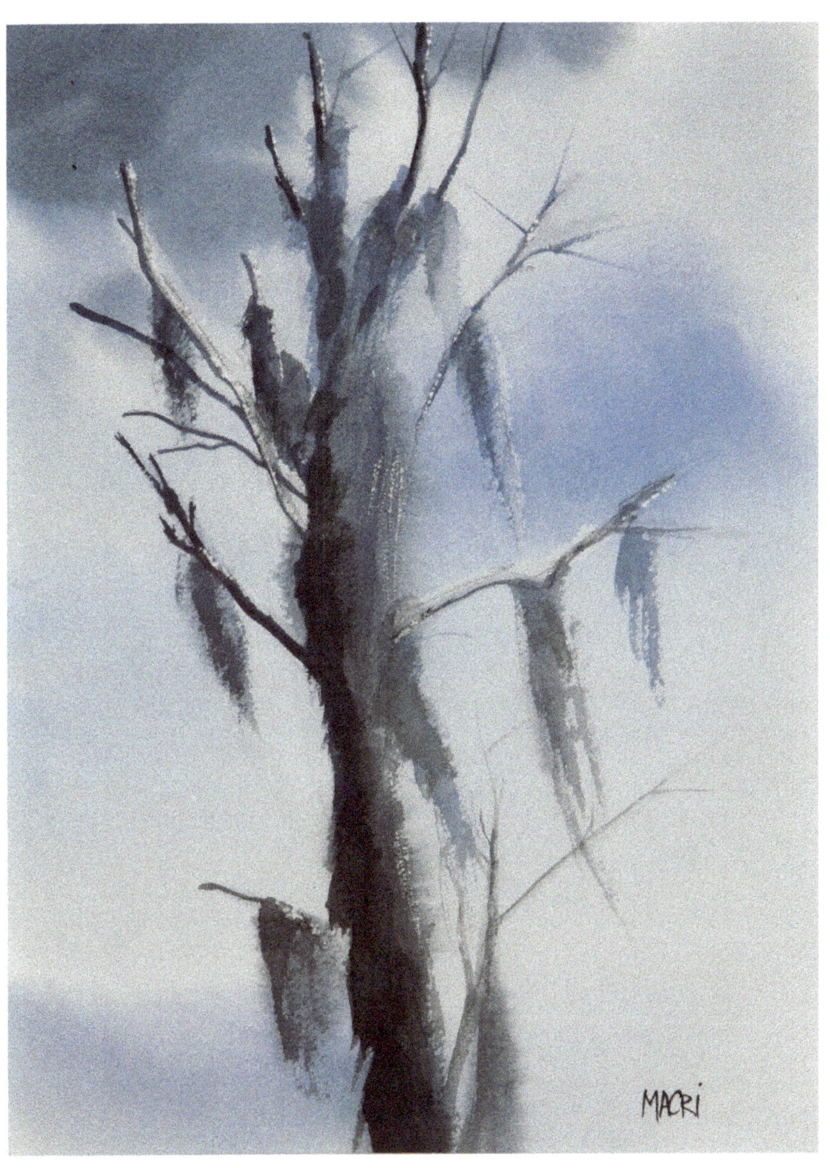

"Mossy Tree"

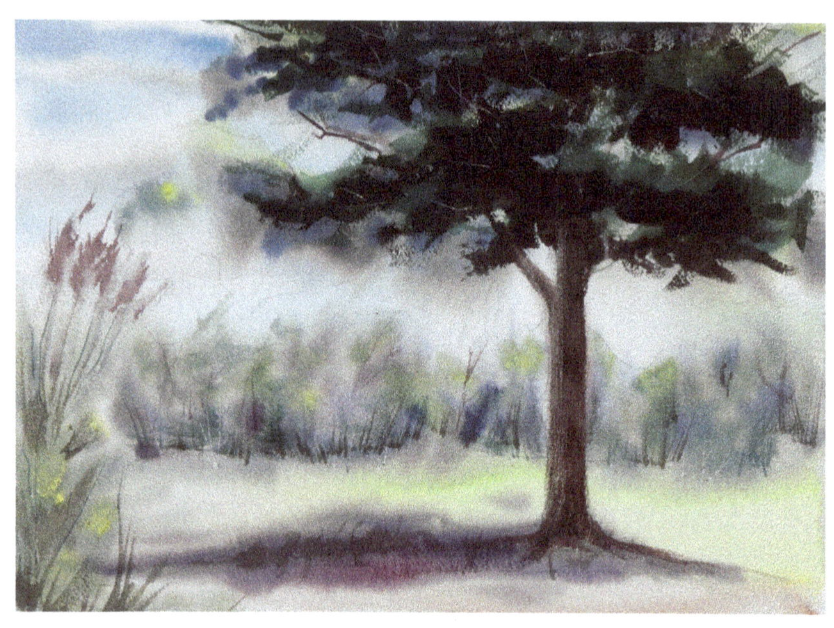

"Treaty Park"

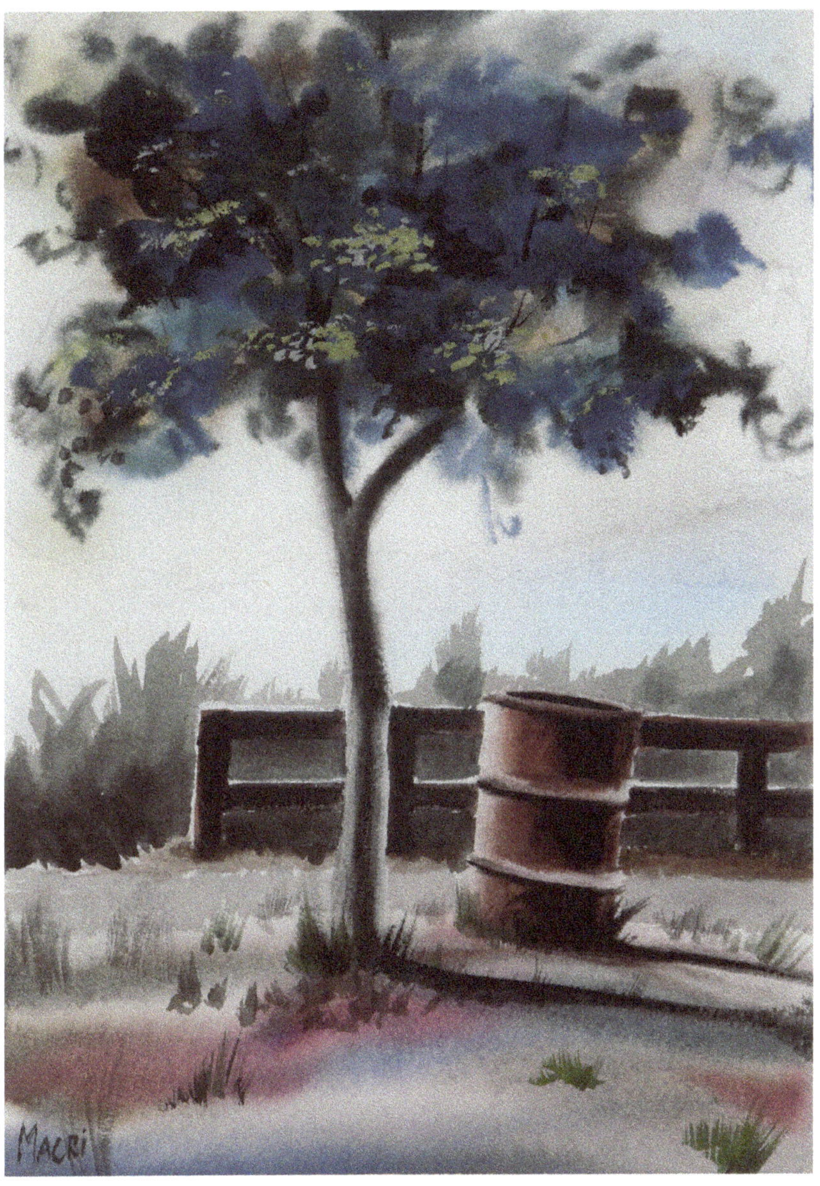

"Treaty Park 2"

Along US-1 and State Rd. 16

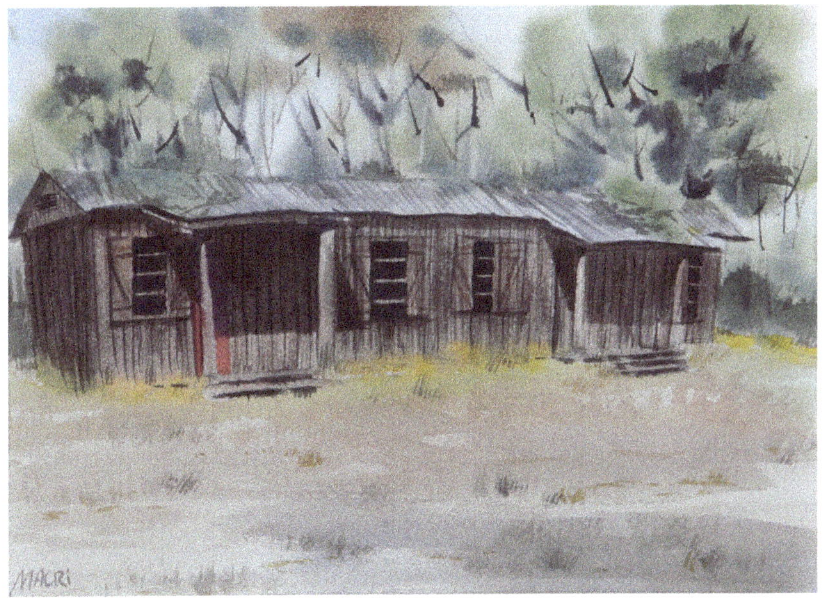

"Abandoned Dwelling off US-1 near the Interstate, January 1, 2002"

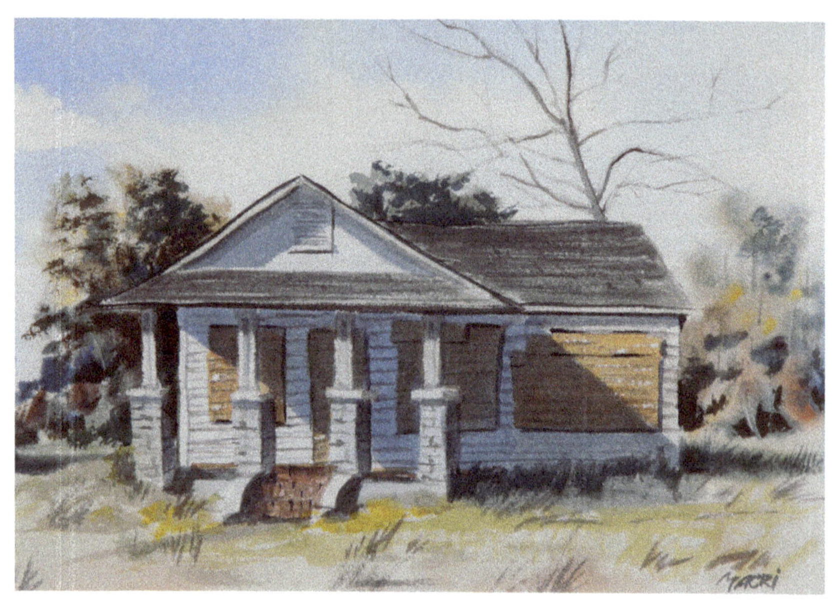

"Abandoned House along US-1"

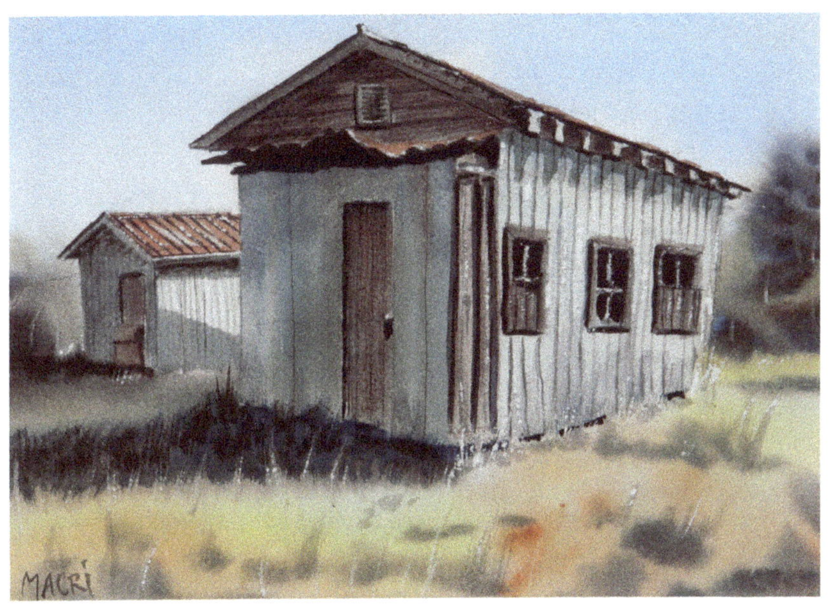

"Abandoned Stand along SR 16, December 18, 2001"

(Demolished)

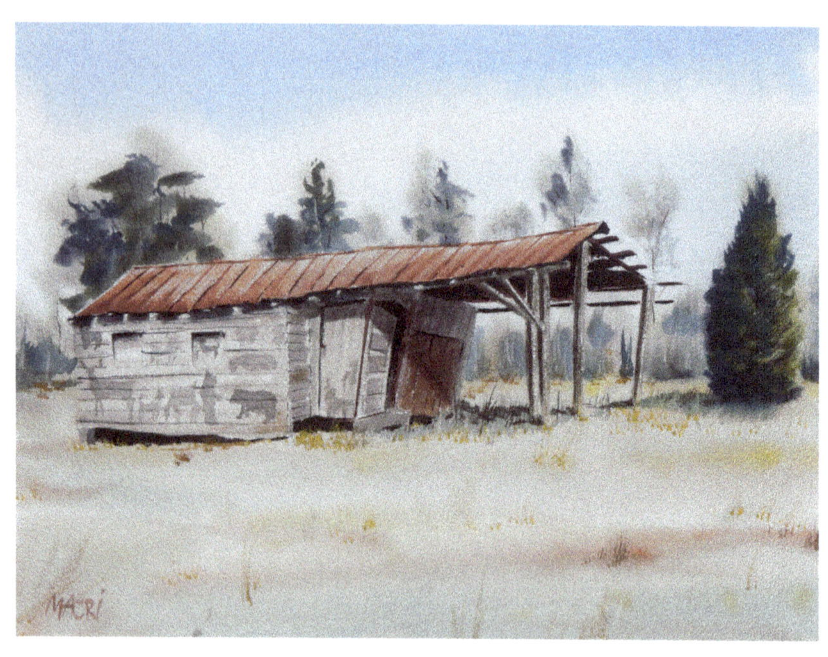

"The Old Petting Zoo along SR 16"
(Demolished)

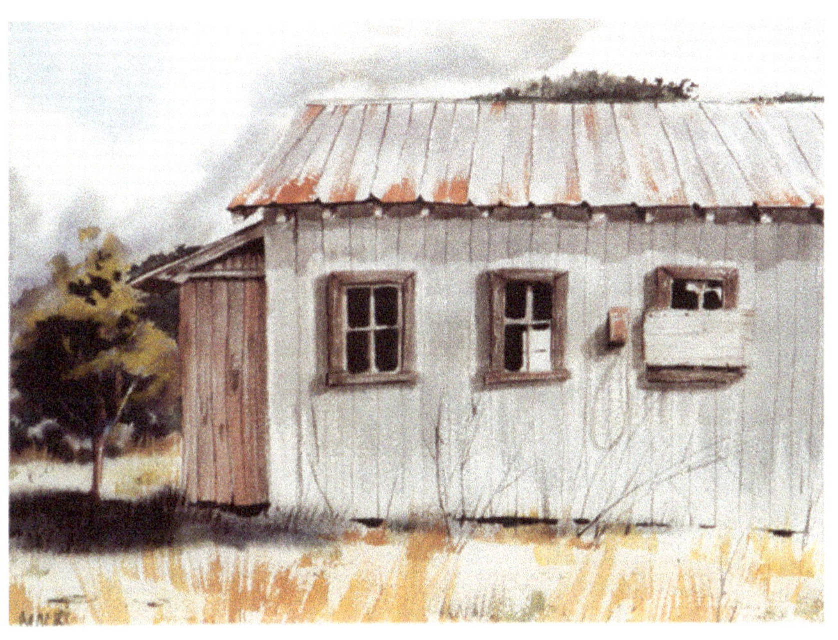

"Shed along SR 16"
(Demolished)

North Beaches

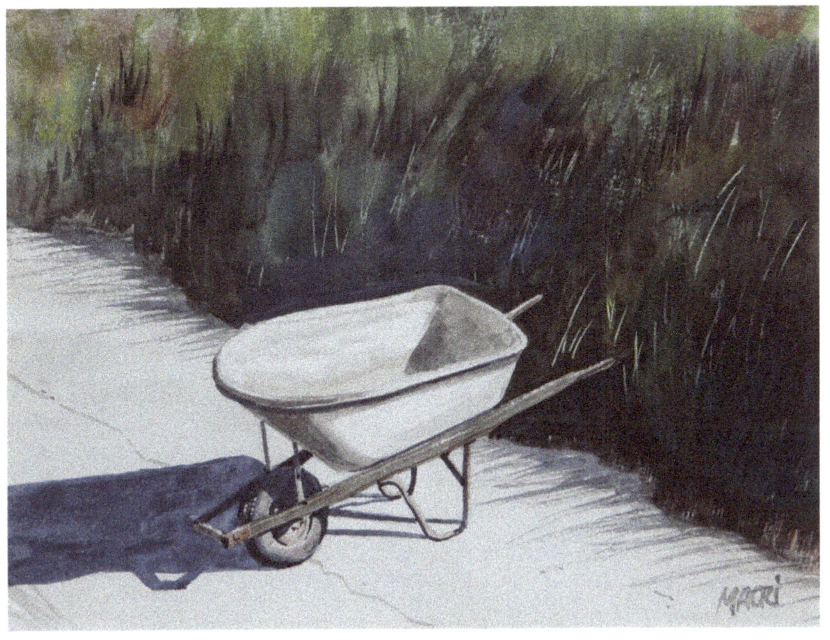

"Wheelbarrow by the Road near Vilano Beach"

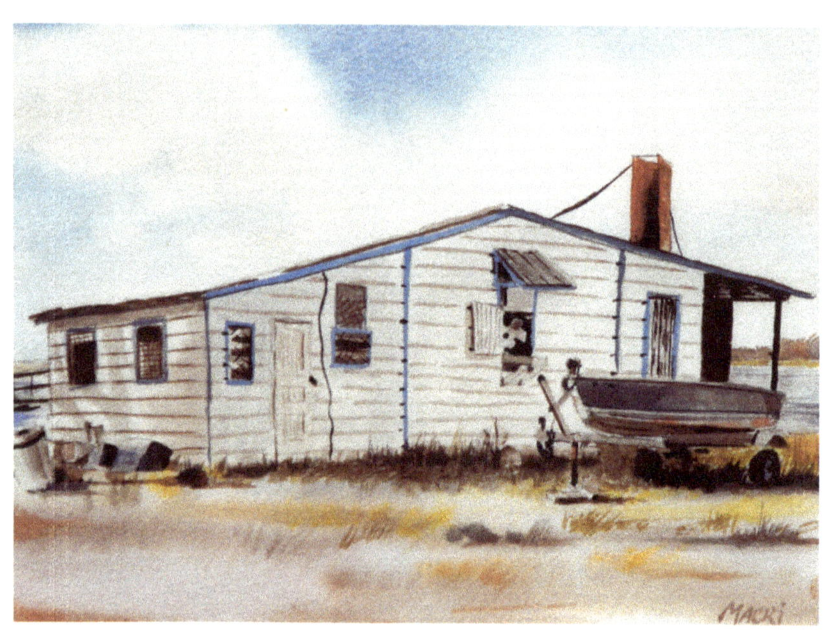

"Rear View of Old Bait House"

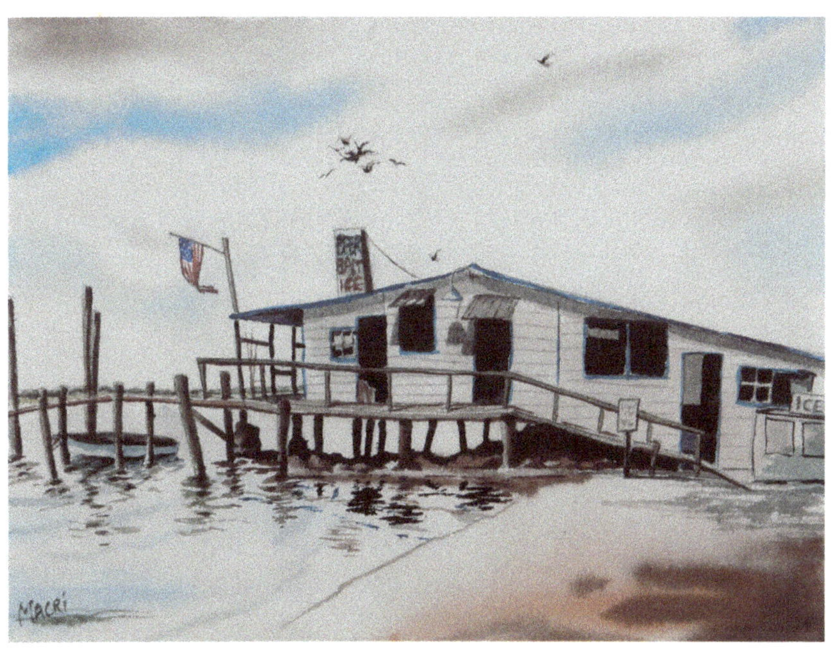

"Front View of Old Bait House on Intracoastal near Vilano Beach"

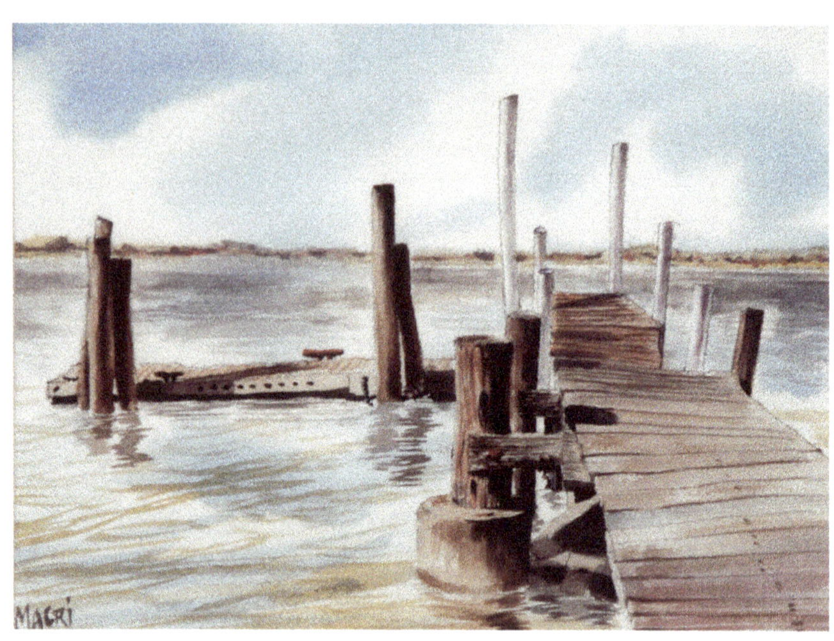

"Small Pier"

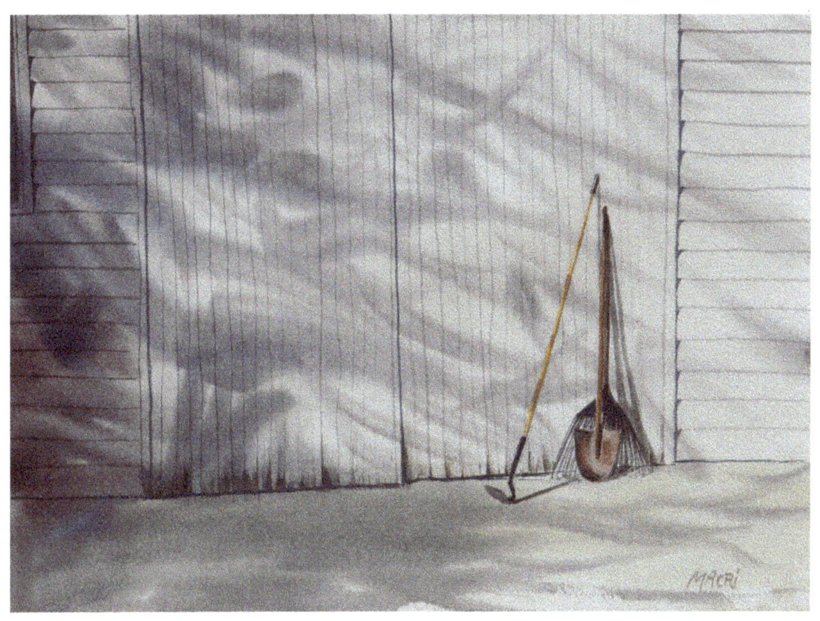

"Garden Tools, Vilano Beach"
(March 2002)

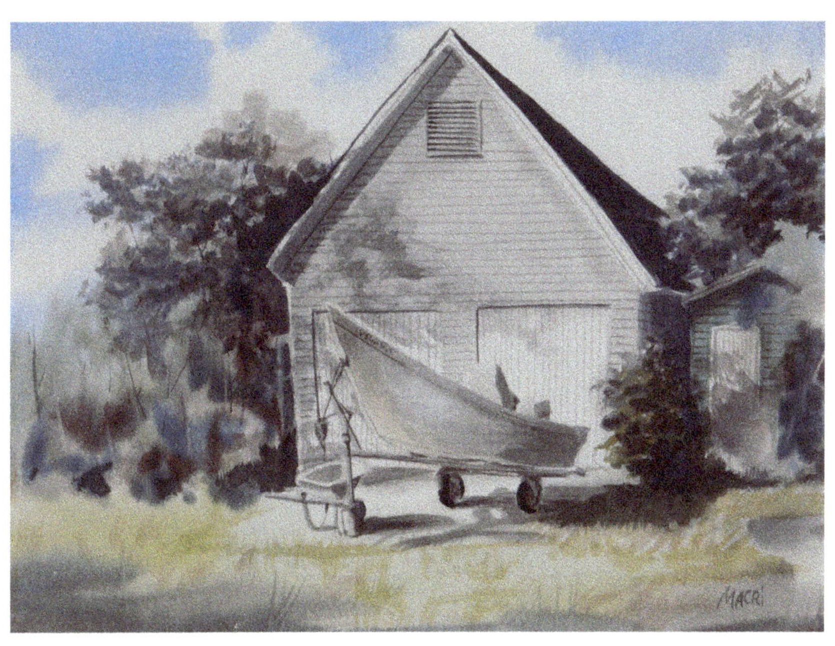

"Boat in Driveway, North Beach"

Downtown

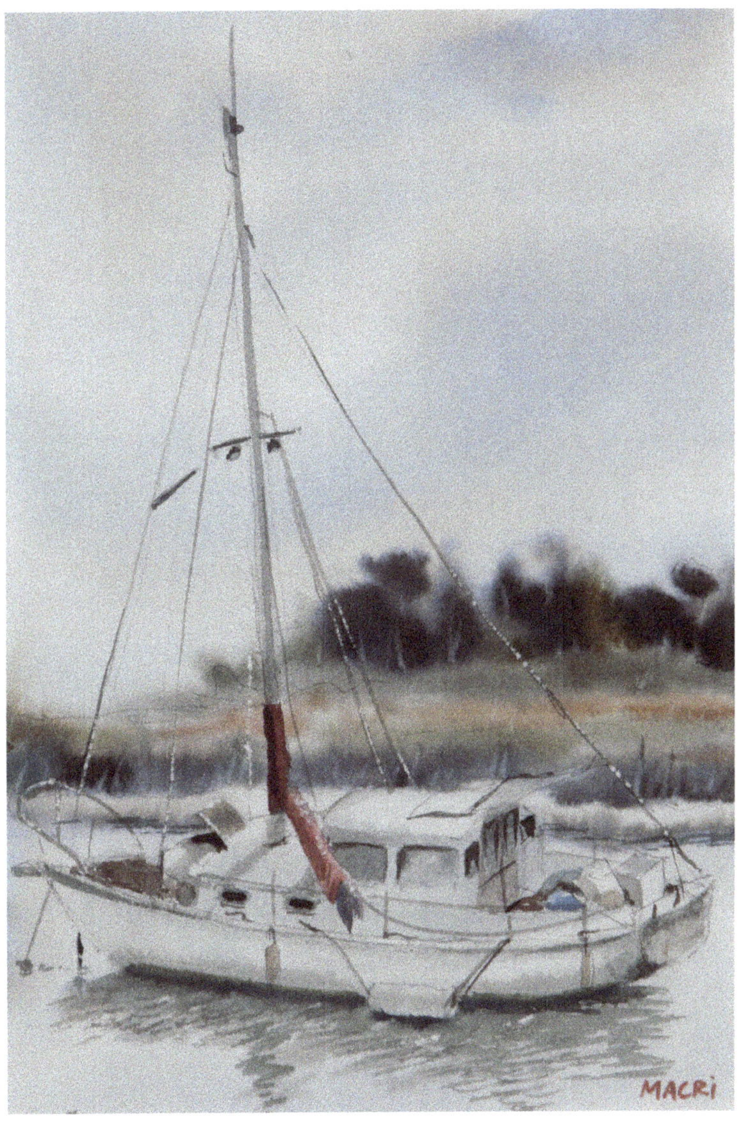

"Boat Study in Mission Park"
(December 16, 2001, 2-3 p.m.)

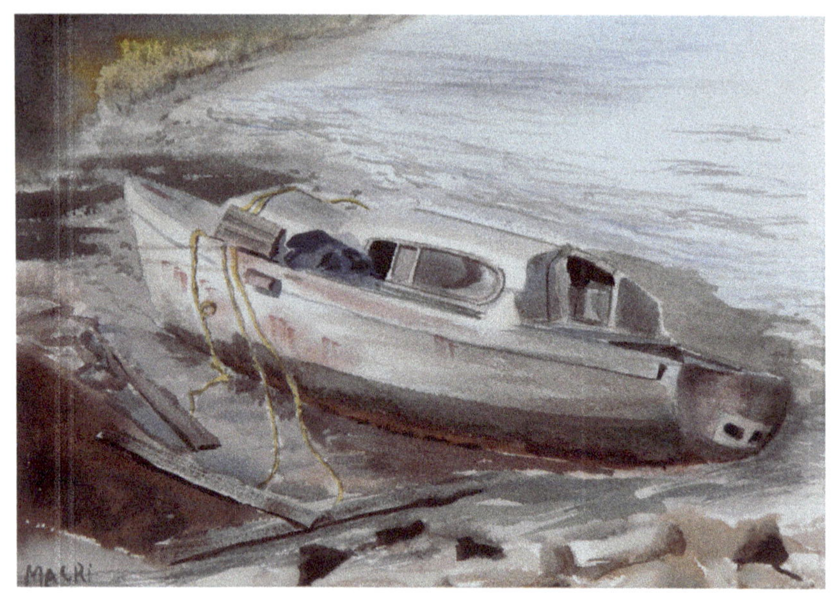

"Abandoned Boat in Mission Park"
(December 15, 2001, 2:30-3:30 p.m.)

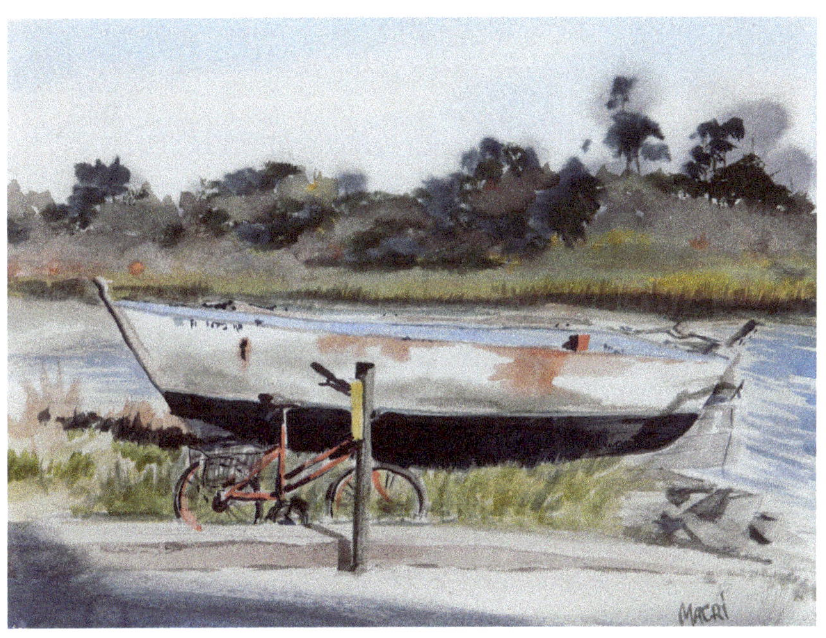

"Boat and Bike along Downtown Waterfront"

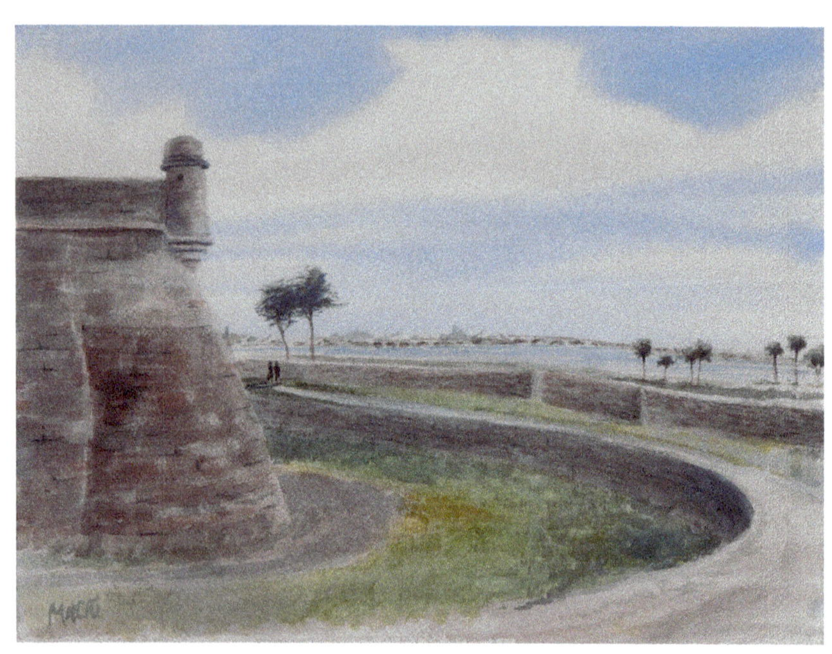

"Castillo de San Marcos"

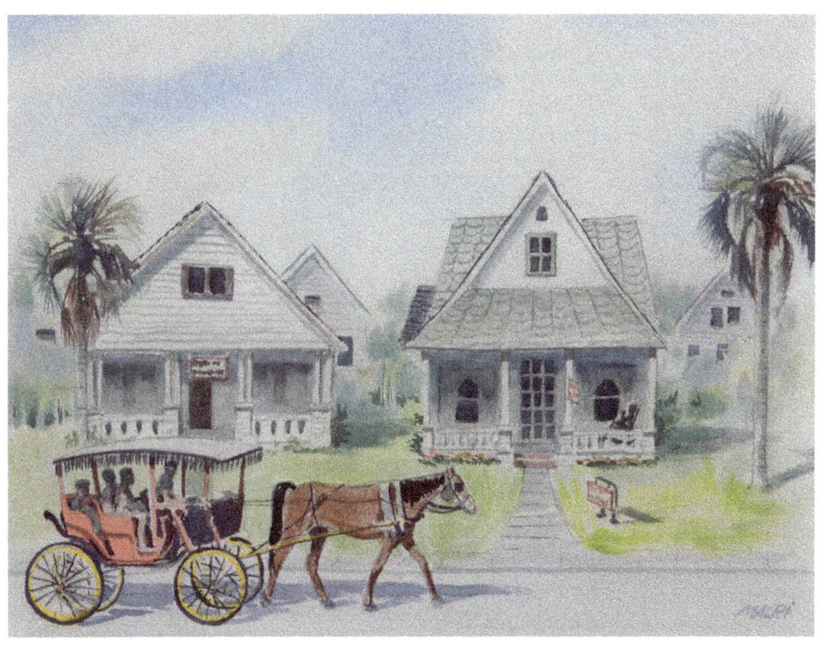

"Horse and Carriage"

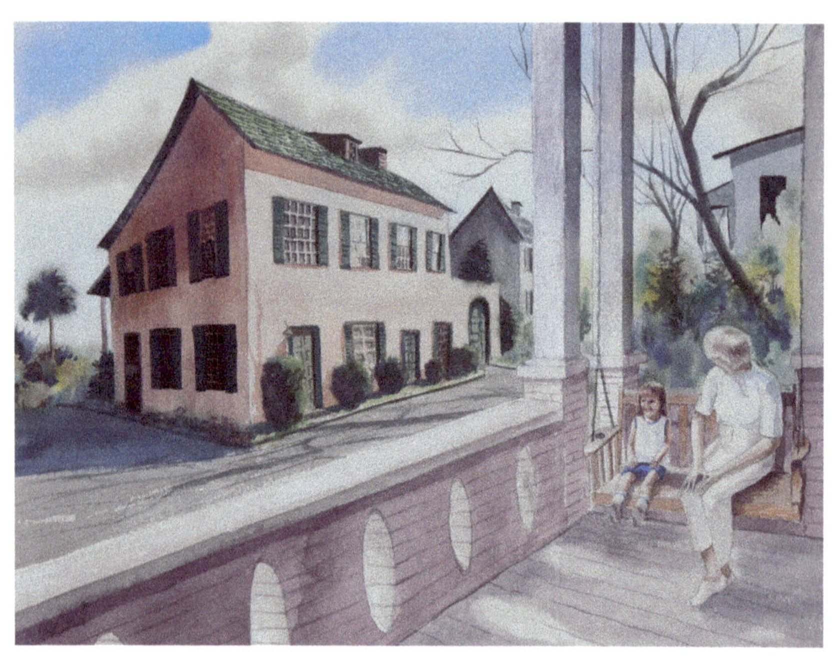

"House on Marine Street"

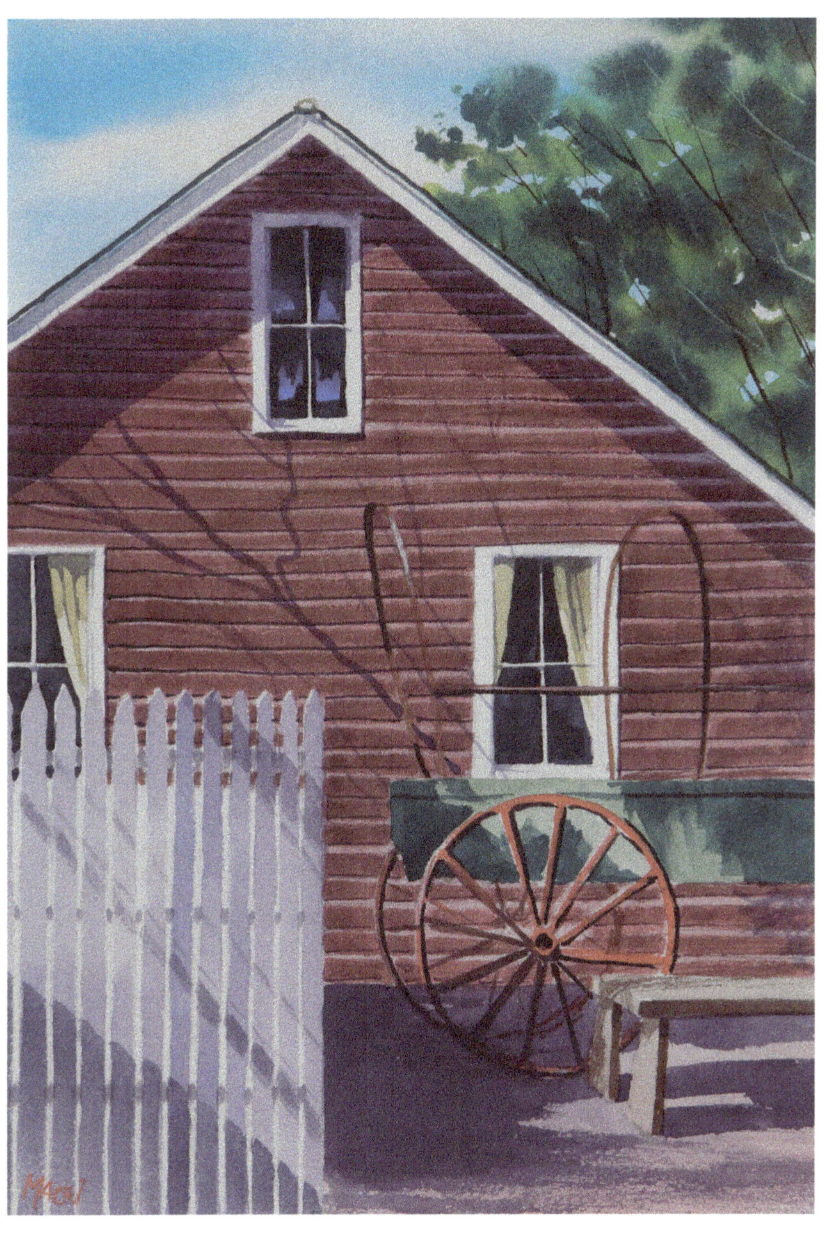

"Star General Store"

(Est. 1899)

Dow House Museum Collection

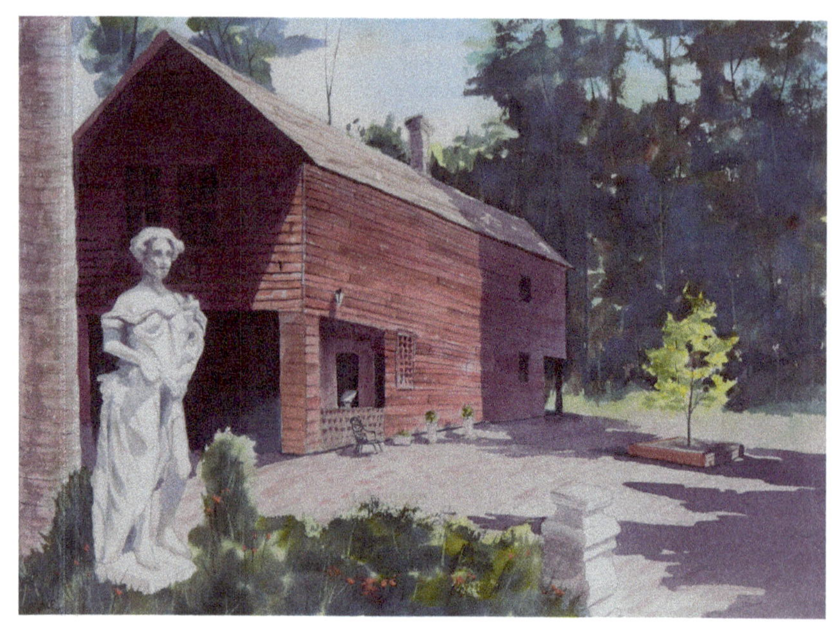

"Carpenter House"
(Built in 1910 by John Henry for his widowed sister-in-law)
Dow House Museum Collection

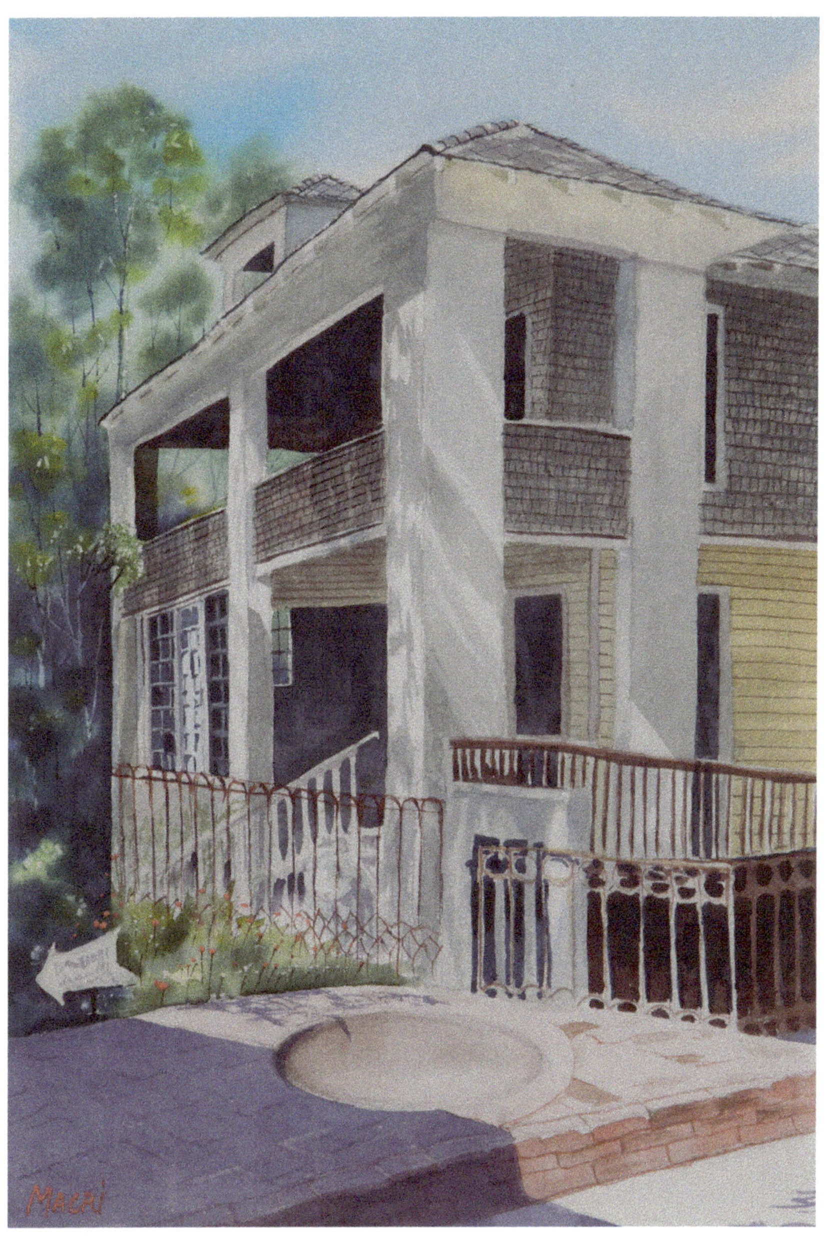

"The Spear Carriage House"

(Built by Andrew Spear in 1899, with second floor added in 1904 by John Henry)

Dow House Museum Collection

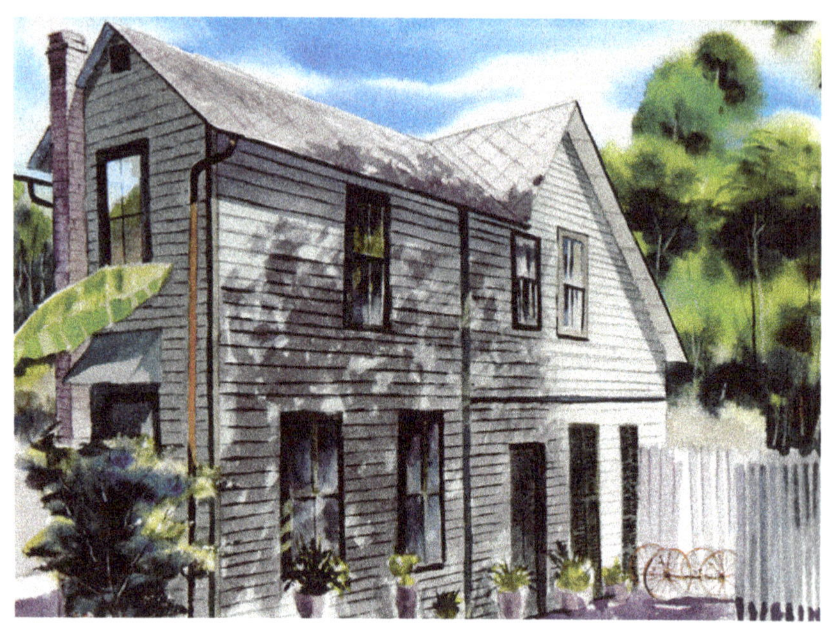

"Howell's House"
(William Dean Howell's winter home, built in 1907)
Dow House Museum Collection

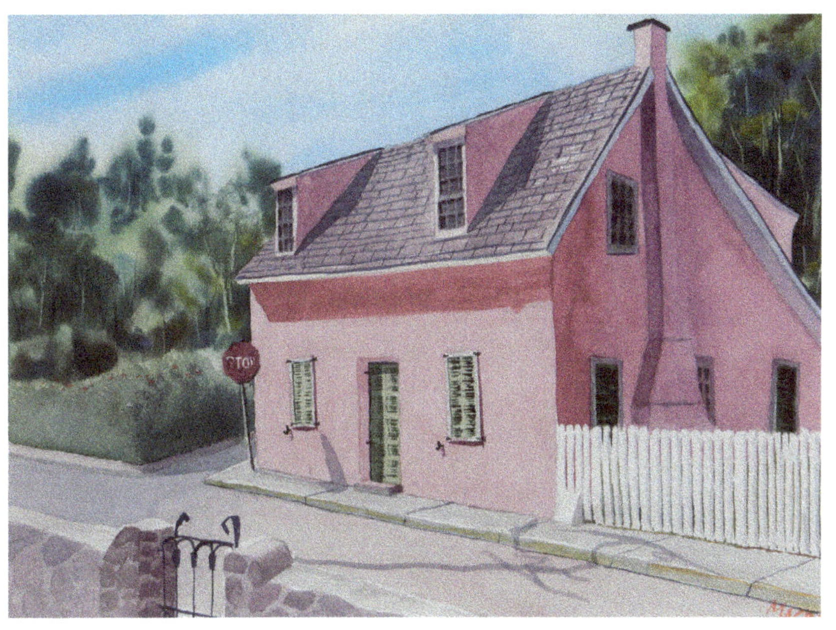

"Prince Murat House at 250 St. George Street"
(Built under a Spanish land grant by Antonio Huretos in 1792)
Dow House Museum Collection

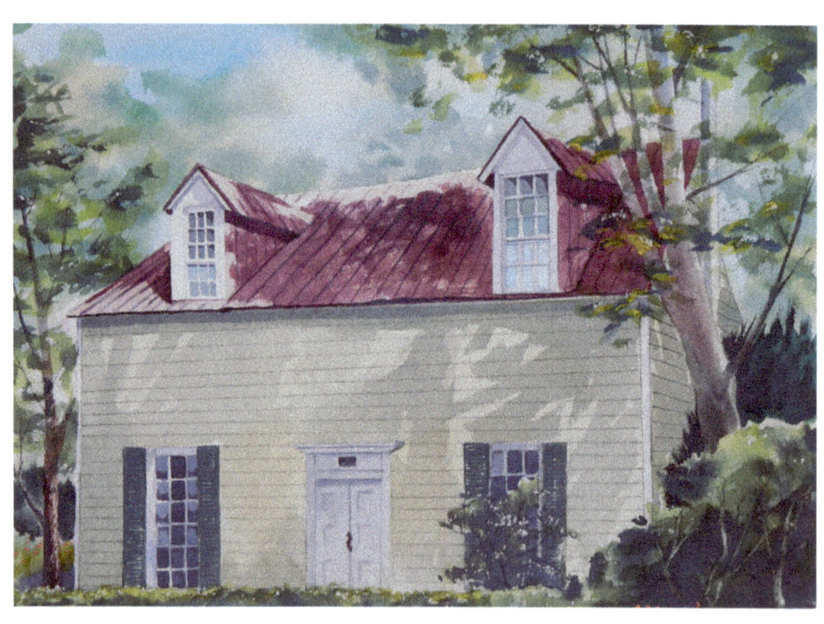

"The Dow House"
(Built in 1839 by the Canova Family)
Dow House Museum Collection

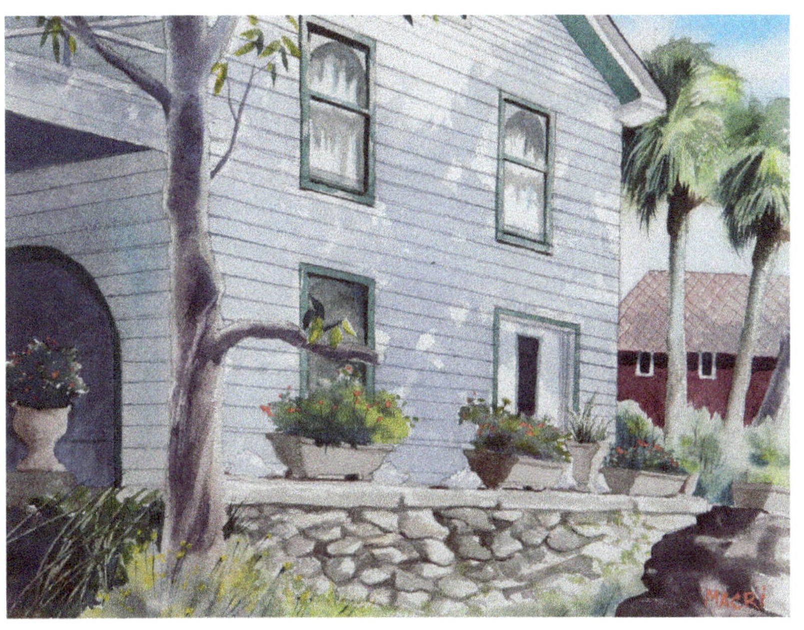

"Worcester House"

(Built by John Henry for his new bride in 1906)

Dow House Museum Collection

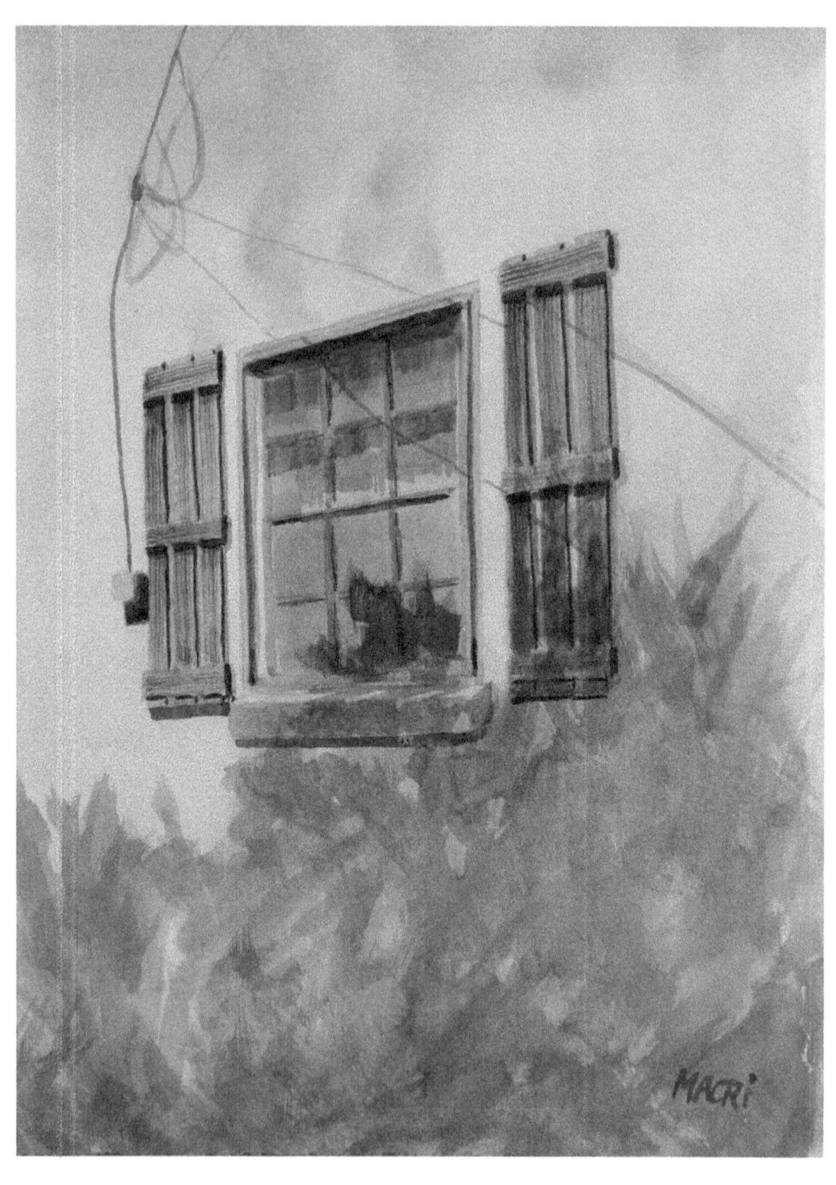

"Canova de Medici's house window with shadows"

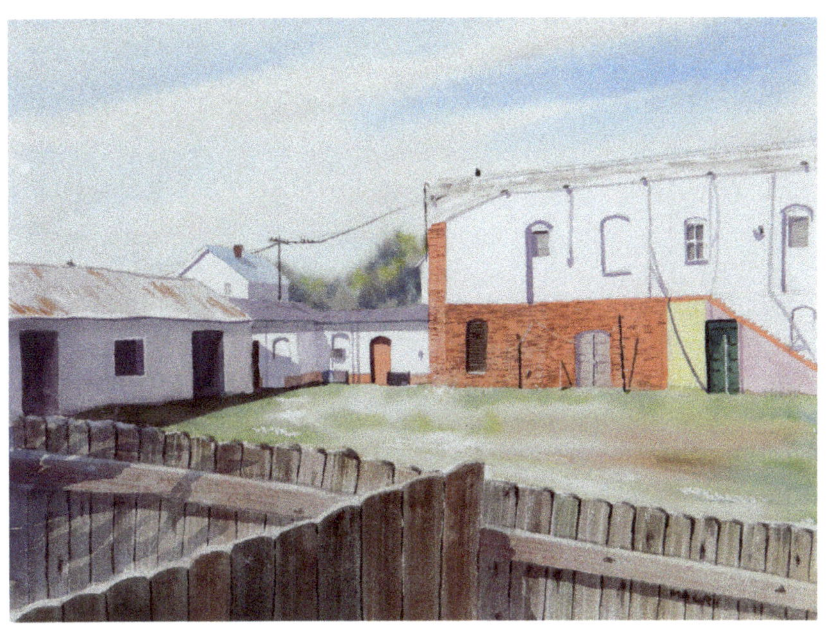

"Shared Back Lot off King Street and Davis Street"

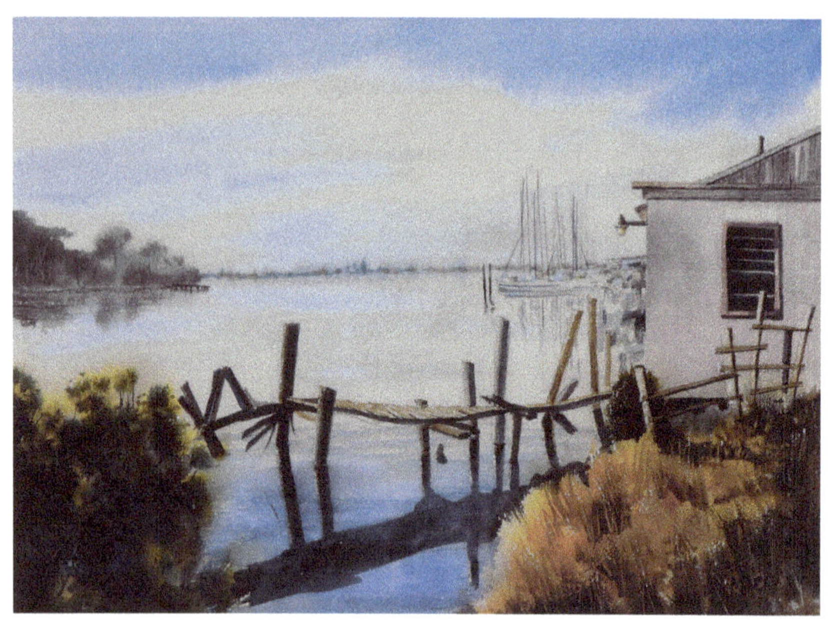

"Fazio's Bait House near the San Sebastian River Bridge"

(Demolished)

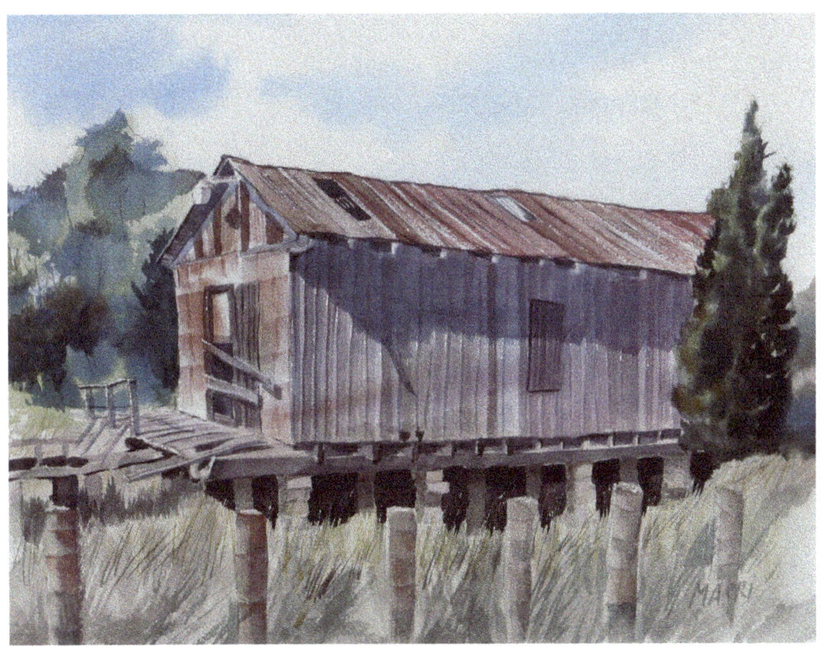

"Abandoned Bait House off King Street near San Sebastian River Bridge"
(Demolished)

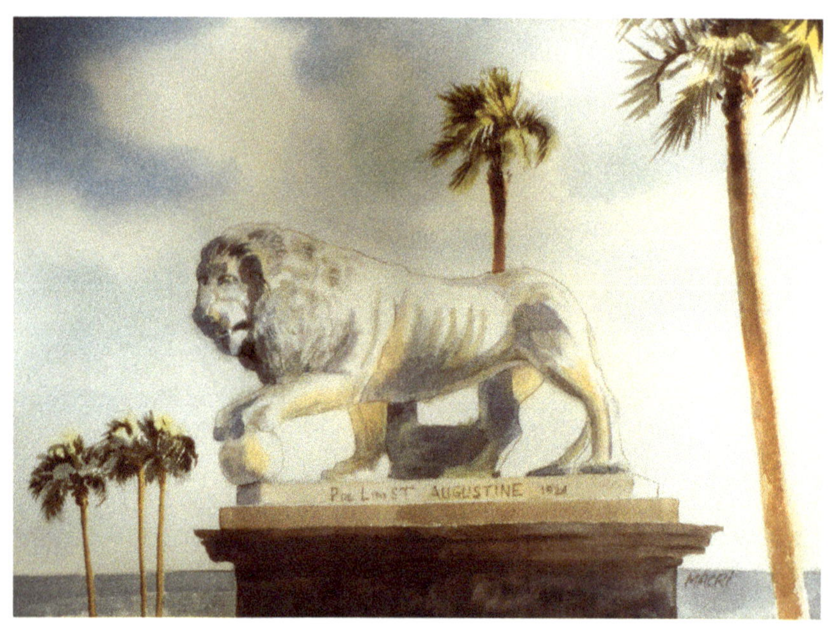

"Lion"

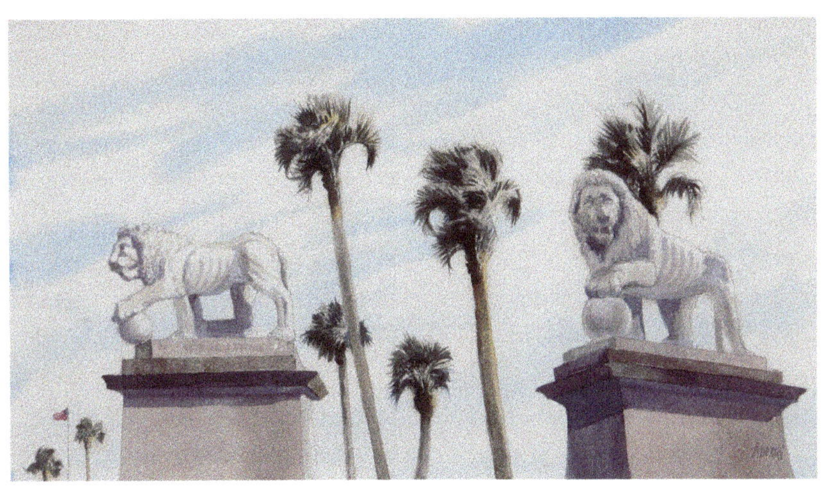

"Lions at the Bridge"

Anastasia Island

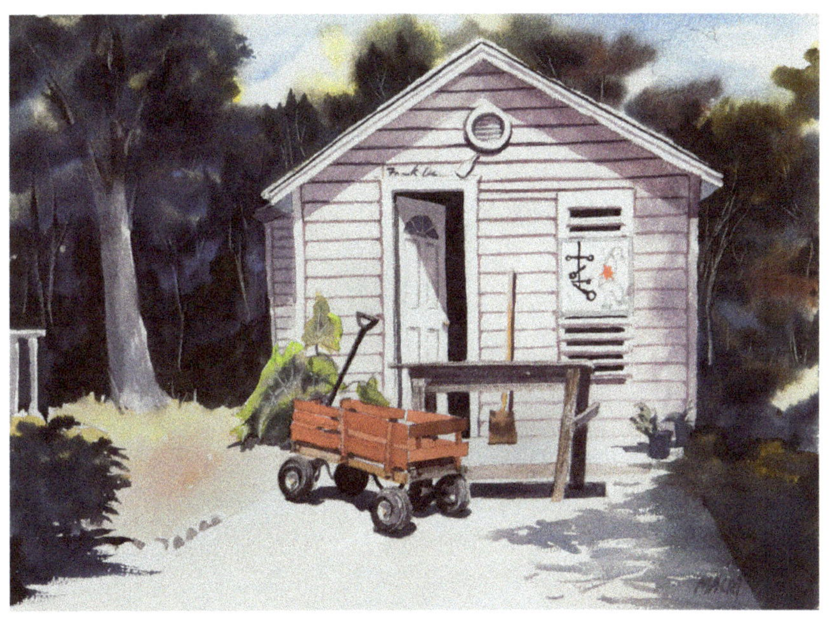

"Billy Matlock's Art Studio"

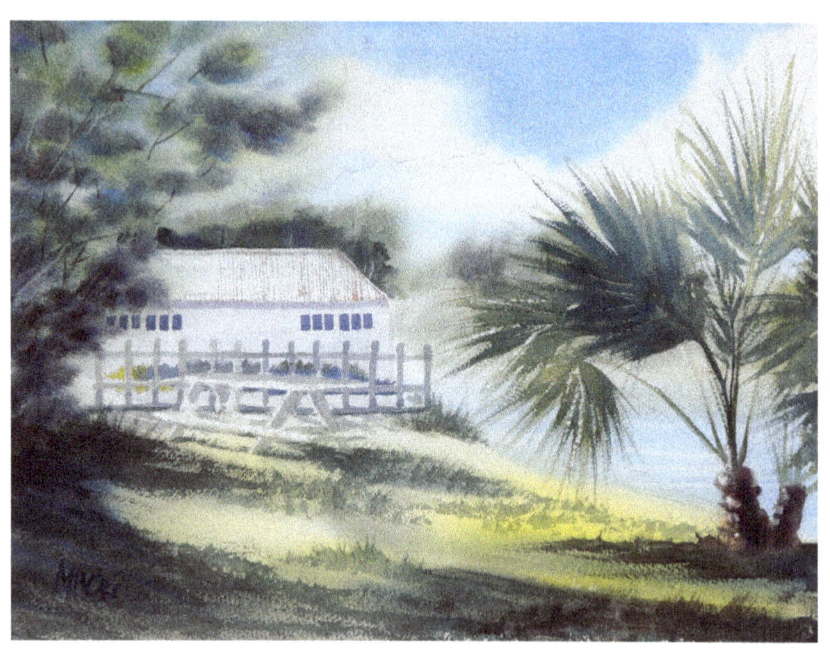

"Lighthouse Park"

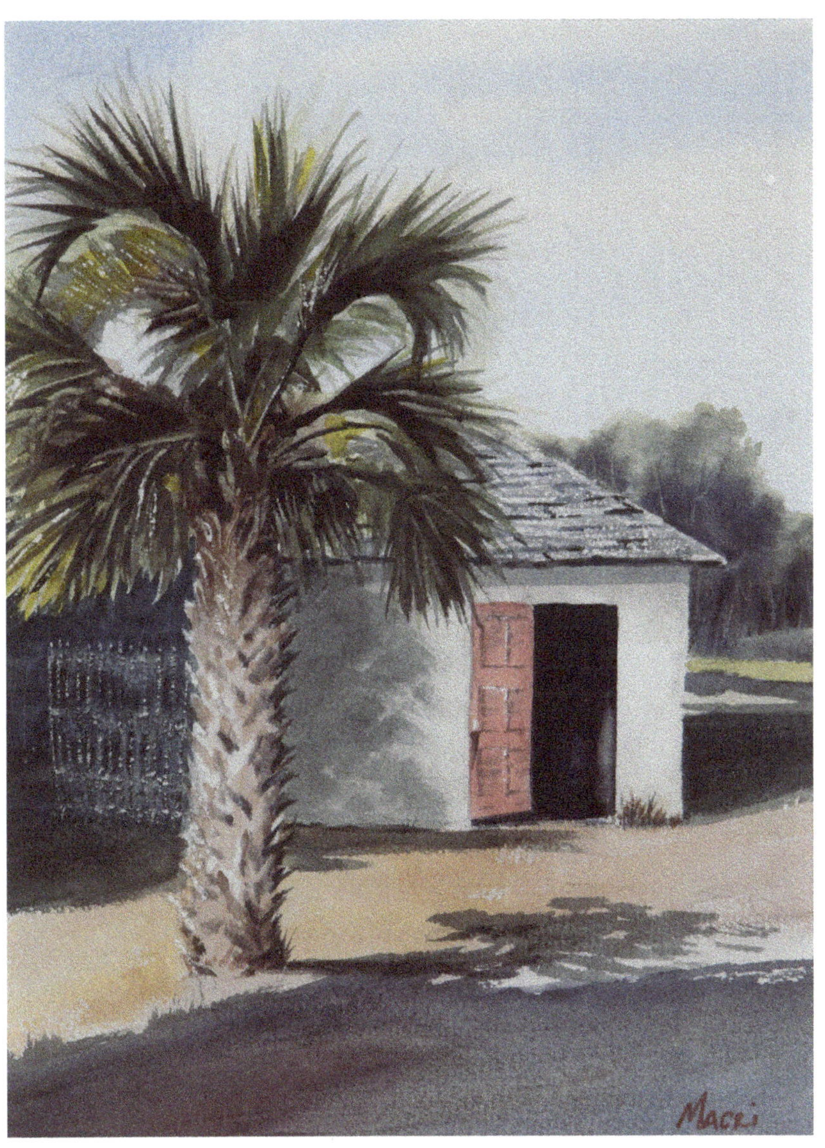

"Work-Building in Lighthouse Park"

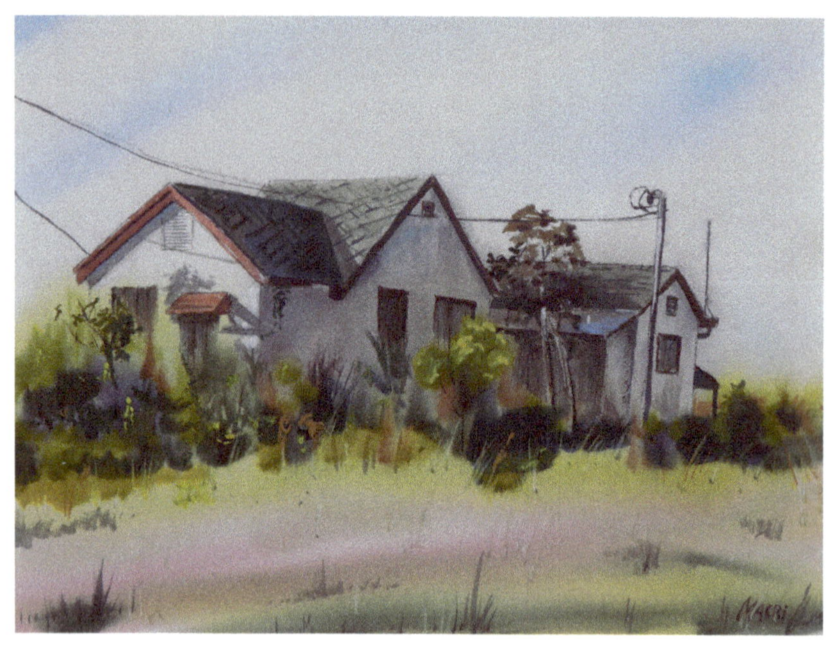

"Abandoned Cottages along A1A, November 2001"

(Demolished except for one now used for storage at public park)

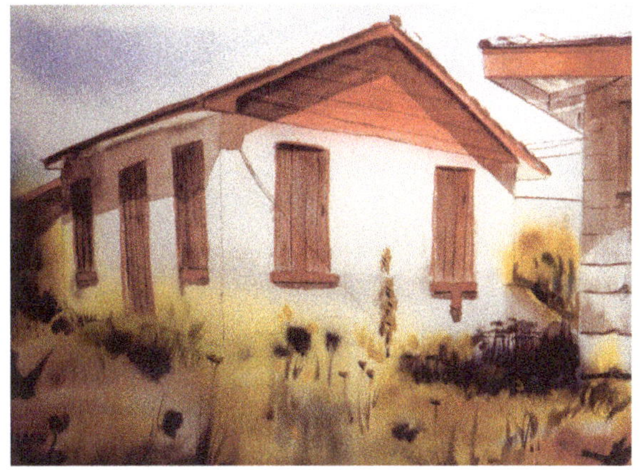

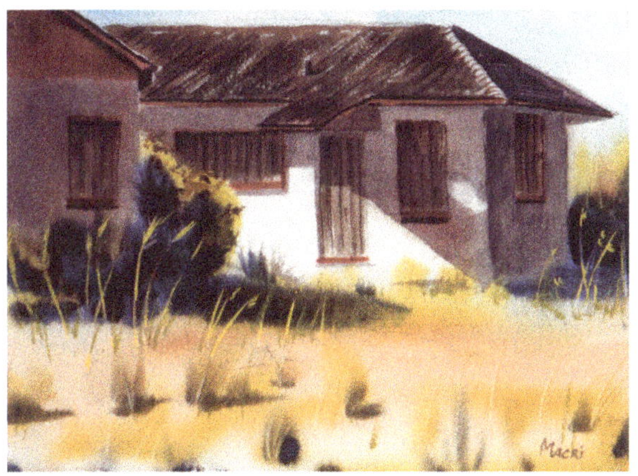

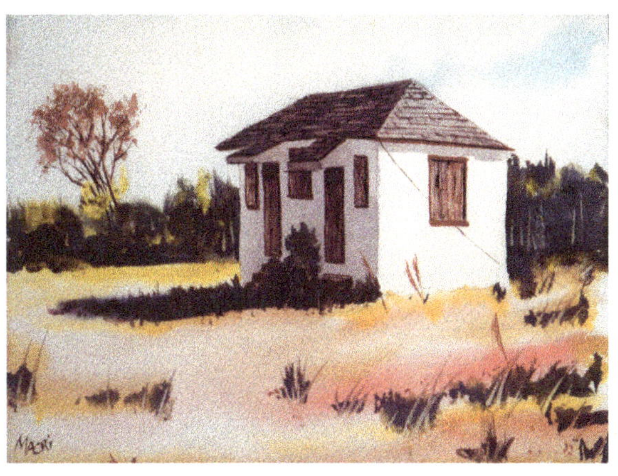

"Abandoned Beach Cottages along A1A"

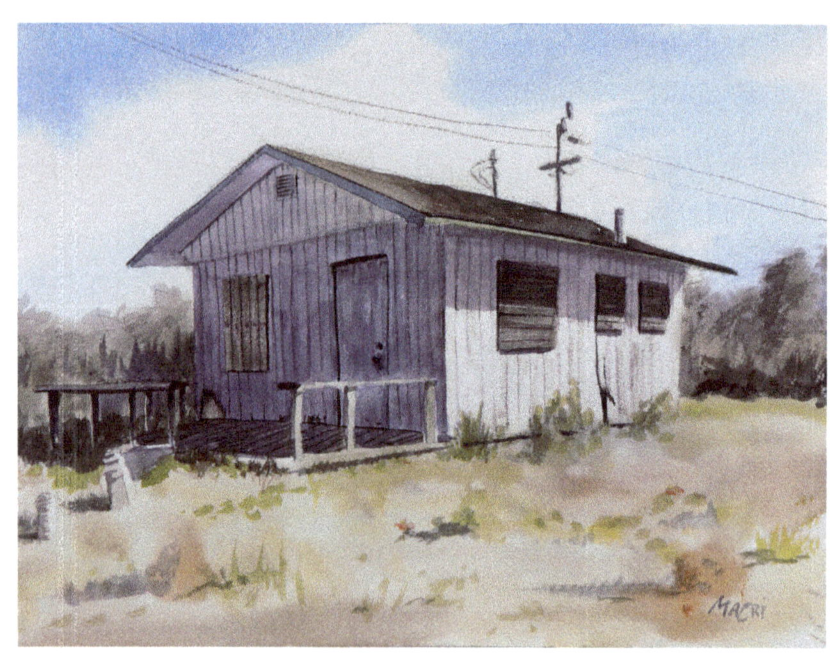

"Treasure Beach Shack"
(Demolished)

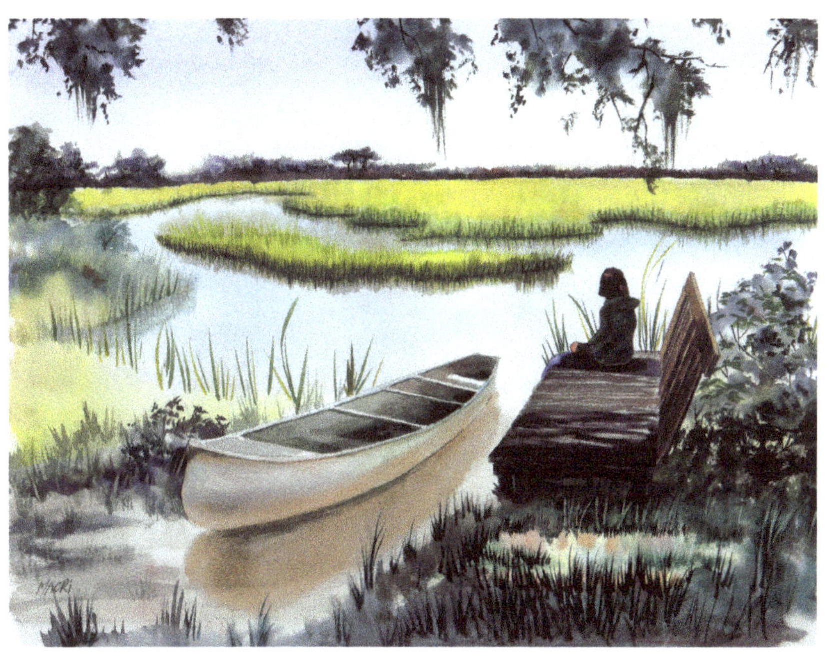

"Self Portrait on the Intracoastal"

Further South

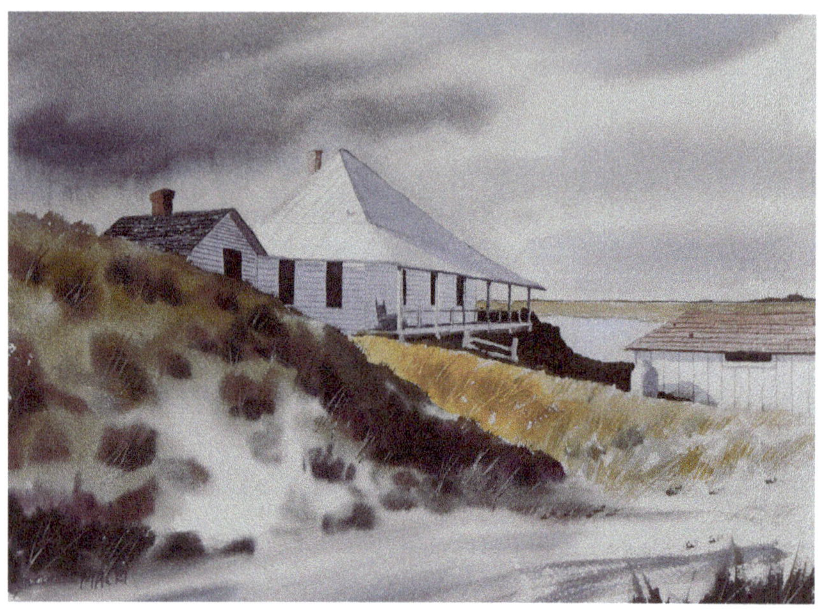

"The Lodge along A1A at Summer Haven"

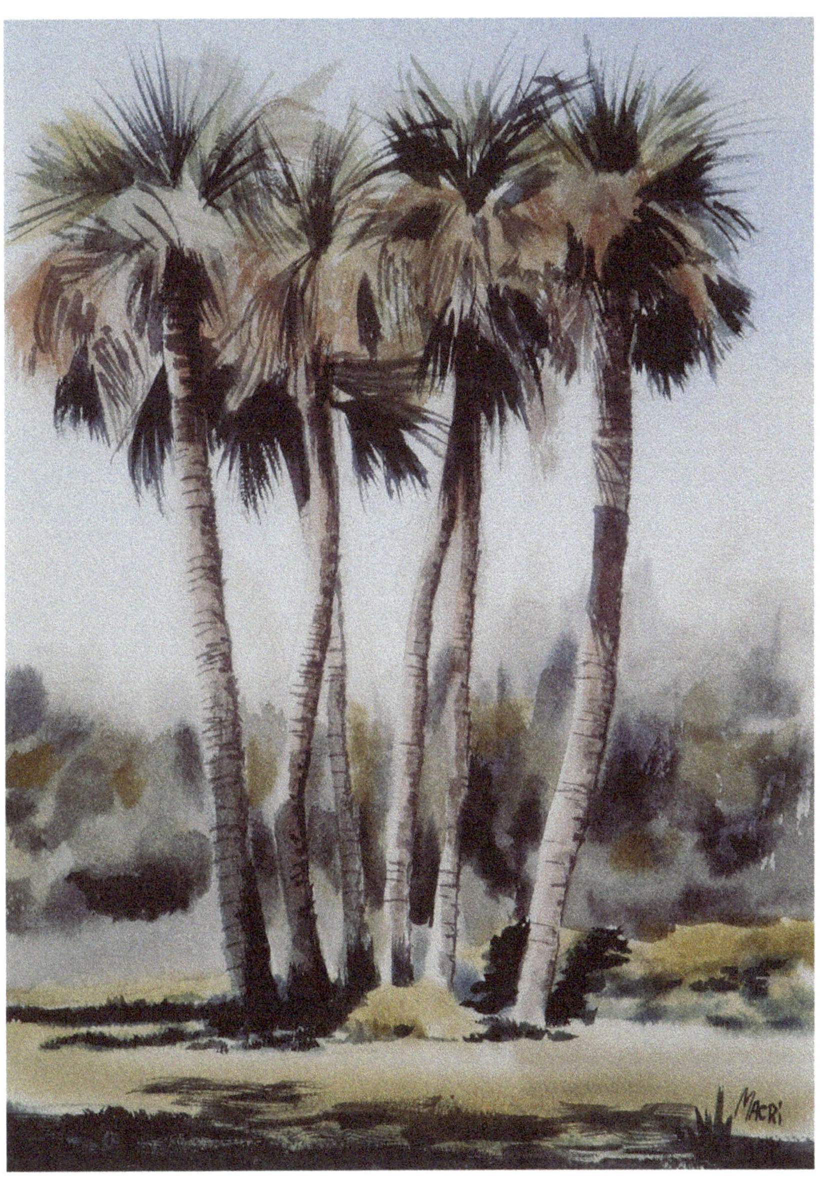

"Palms in Washington Oaks State Park along A1A"

Cooksey's Campground

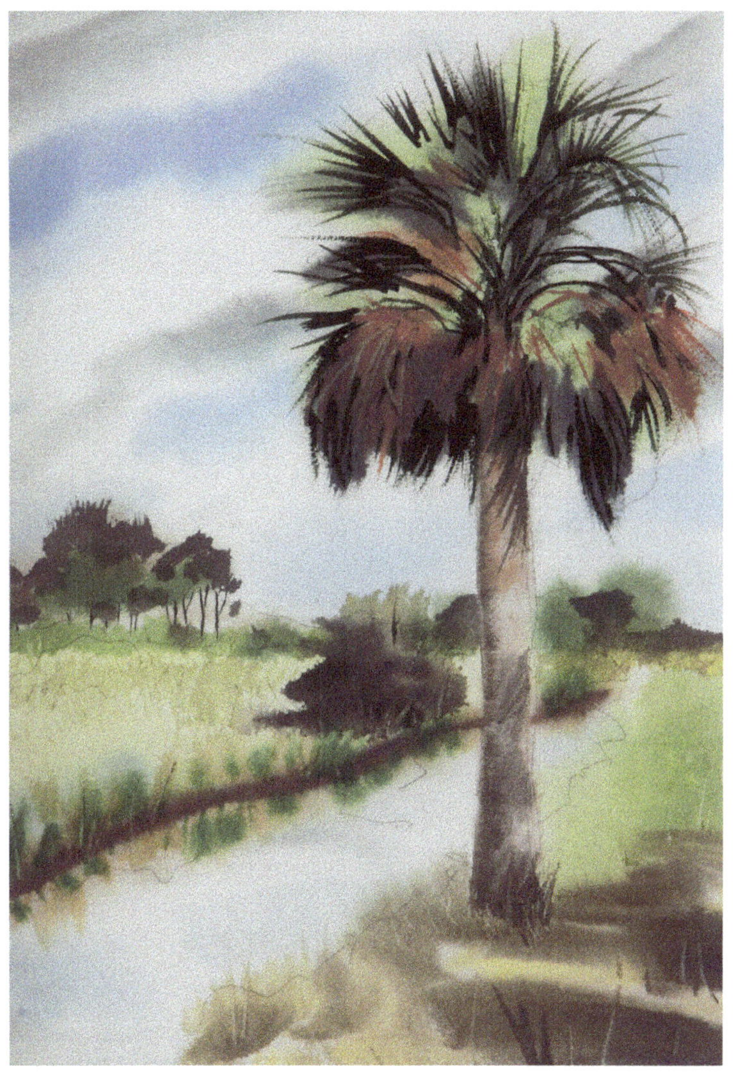

"Lone Palm in Cooksey's"

(Gone)

STEP LIGHTLY, PAINT QUICKLY

The last time I went there, I thought it would surely be my last. Informed by an official-looking man in uniform driving a go-cart that I was trespassing, I was kindly told to leave. I was going to be more careful this time. I found a new, secluded path leading into Cooksey's Campground at the end of a new housing development. I knew that all too soon the sound of bulldozers and straining machinery would fill the air, as the vast wild acreage known as Cooksey's had been sold. The natural vista that I had only recently discovered, full of towering pine and oak trees, rugged paths leading to ponds surrounded by wildflowers, the sound of birds filling the air, would be forever lost to another development. I wanted to capture everything I could of it, in a series of watercolor paintings, before it was permanently altered.

There was no sign of the guard as I crept in at the north end of the property. I stepped up and over the small dune-like berm that separated the end of the road from the beginning of wilderness, and was startled by a rustling in the

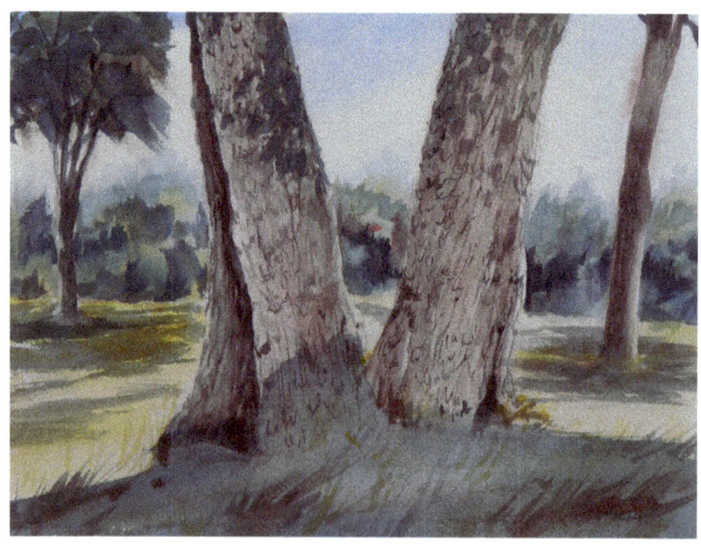

"Base of Trees"

(Gone)

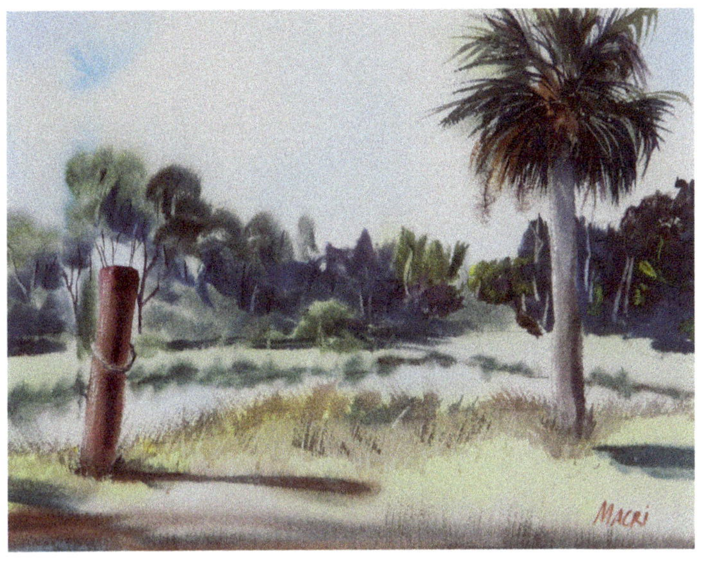

"Lone Palm by the Water, October 2001"
(Gone)

underbrush. I gasped, expecting him to be standing there, ordering me to get out. That last day, he had found me when I was halfway through painting a family of palm trees. I honestly thought I was outside the property lines. I had been shaken from my trance, staring at the way the purple shadows fell across the rough tree trunks, by footsteps in the dry grass. There he stood, an elderly gentleman in khaki pants and shirt, wearing a dark brown cap. He said nothing at first, so that I thought he was just watching me paint. I was used to people stopping to watch as I painted on site. I smiled at him and said something about it being a nice day, and that was when he told me I was trespassing.

"I'm sorry," I said, "I thought I was outside the fence."

"Oh, no. All this land is Mr. Cooksey's. I'm not supposed to let anyone in," he said matter-of-factly. I decided to go for the sympathy card.

"Well, could I at least finish it? It'll only take me about ten minutes."
He hesitated.

"I guess," he said, smiling, almost as if he felt guilty about it all. "But, then you'll have to leave. I'm sorry."

Watching him walk slowly away looking down at the ground, I wondered how he felt about what was going to happen to all this. As I stood up and looked across the untamed vista before me, I suddenly felt indignant. This wasn't my land, but I was angry that it would soon be developed. What would be left that was real if most of our natural land was swallowed up? Every city in Florida was starting to look the same, all the same developments, chain restaurants, and stores. I was also mad at myself. How many times had I driven past all this, all the trees and lush wilderness, and seen nothing but scrub brush and palm trees? Now that I had started taking the time to look, I was seeing things I had never seen before. Every palm tree was different, unique in its own way, and providing homes for the bats that ate those pesky mosquitoes, every invaluable oak throwing cool shade across the earth while offering nesting for

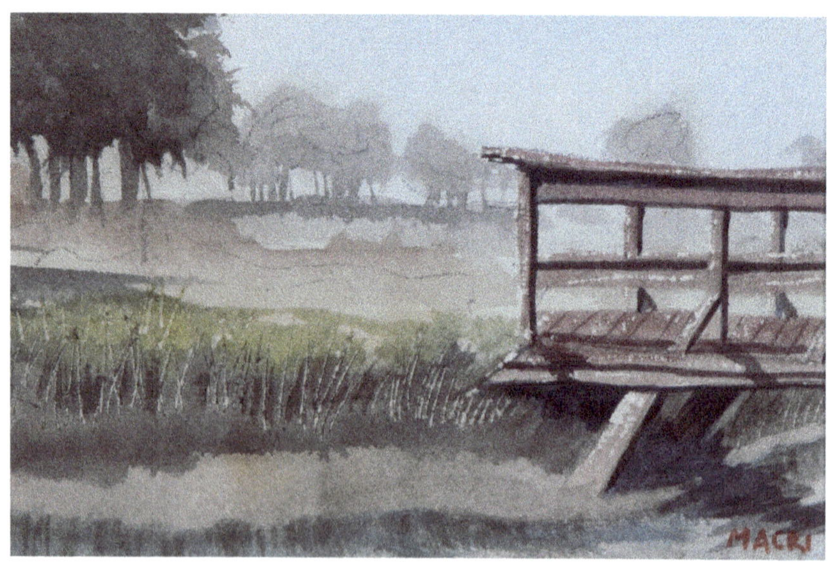

"Small Bridge"

(Gone)

the birds. Each path seemed to trace its way through a wonderland dotted with ponds and I wanted to paint everything. It all suddenly looked like paradise.

As I walked deeper into the elegantly shaped foliage, clusters of trees cast shadows across the golden grass, bending in the gentle breeze to resemble the

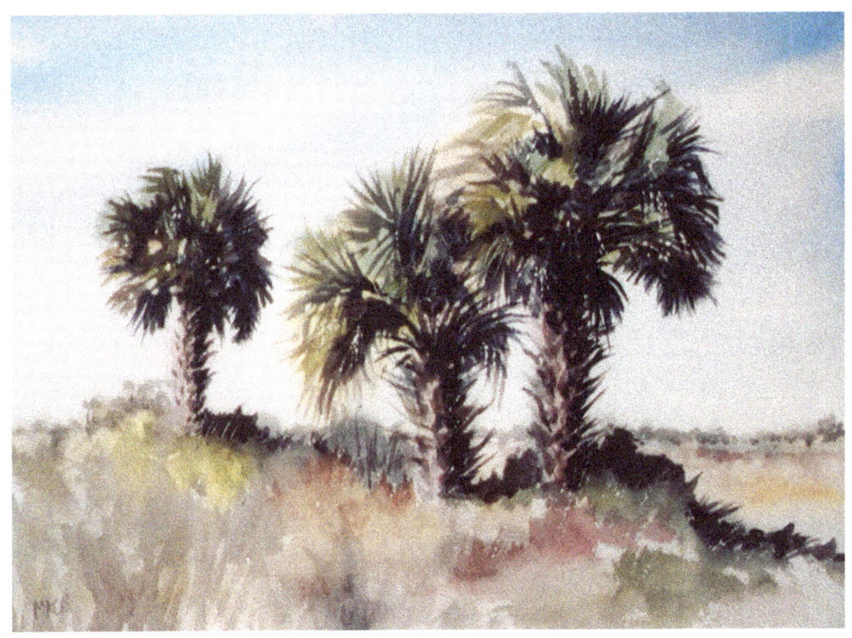

"Three Palms"
(Gone)

fur of some fluffy dog. I had to stop and decide what to paint first. The light was changing with every passing second and would appear very different within thirty minutes. I had to choose, and now — when the shadows stretched out, touching that clump of palmetto, as the changing light brought the hue and value of the grass to a deeper, richer intensity. As I looked to the south, the decision was made. A sand dune rose up in front of me, overlooking the lake that shimmered like diamonds in the afternoon sun, and stepping up onto it brought a quiet explosion of joy within me. I dropped my paintbox onto the

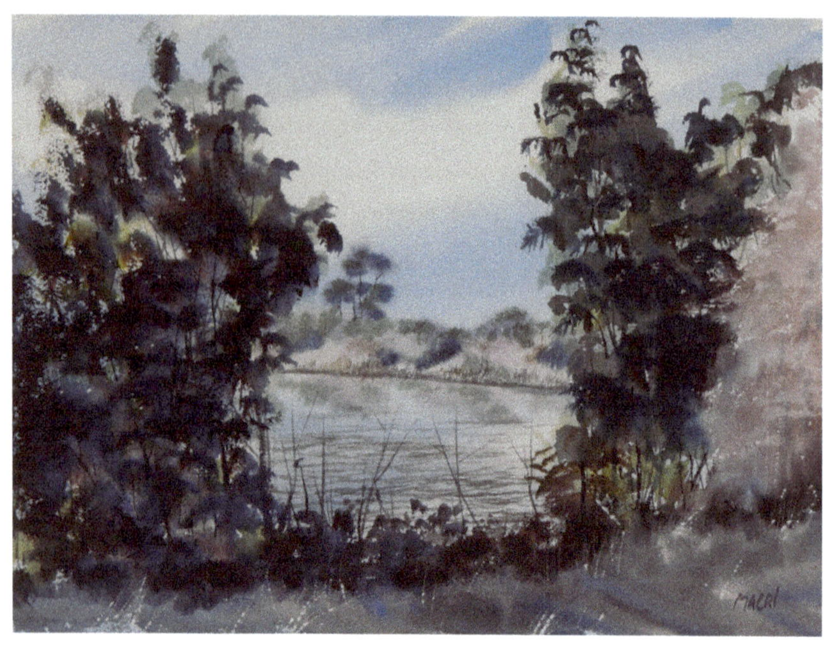

"The Last Painting of Cooksey's Campground, February 15, 2003"
(Gone)

soft yielding sand, my paintbrushes trembling inside their tray in anticipation.

I sat down, took a deep breath, and began to sketch a setting unmarred by human existence and found a small simple happiness. I wanted to shout, "Look! Look at this, will you? Can't we just leave it this way, forever, for everyone to experience?" There will be nothing to soothe the soul or quicken the heartbeat of any human or animal in any composition of new houses, in controlled artificial grandeur and manicured lawns saturated with fertilizer and pesticides.

Right now, all I could do was try in my own way to save what I could by recording some of it by painting. It was the first day of February, and the colors around me seemed to be vibrating in the depths of winter. That was when I sensed imminent failure. How could I ever hope to capture all this? I could never transfer the colors, the crisp verdant smell in the air, the graceful ochre reeds softly leaning in the sunlight dancing on the deep azure water, the song of the birds chirping in the swaying trees, the warmth of the sunlight on my pale skin. The soft pink of the billowing treetops beyond, the evergreens, would simply translate to something contrived beneath my incapable human hand. But I began to paint. And I lost myself.

An hour passed like a minute, and I finally stood, feeling the stiffness in my legs. Placing the painting down on the yielding grass, I heard it: the whir of the

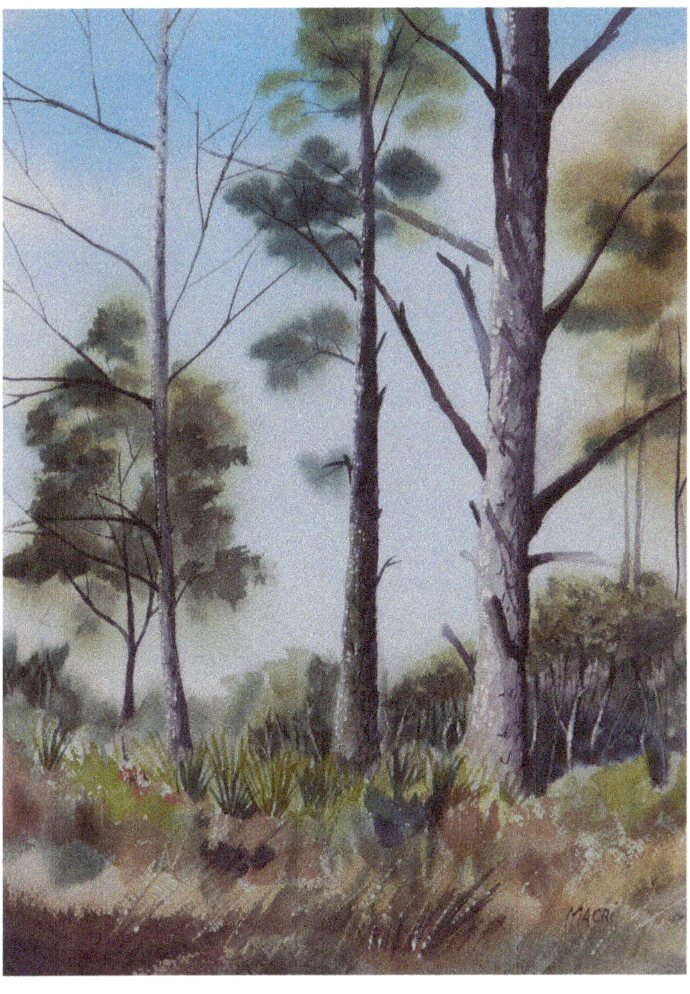

"Pine Study"

(Gone)

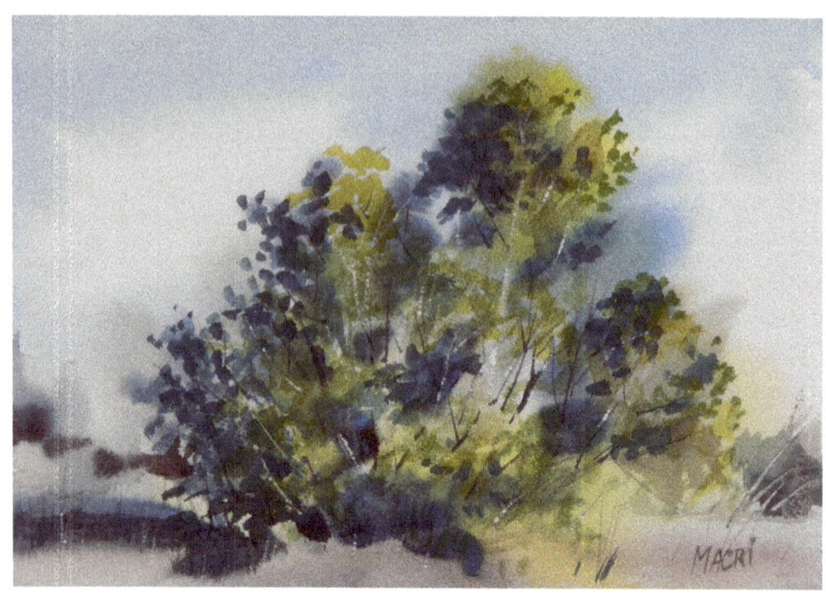

"Foliage in Cooksey's, January 13, 2002"
(Gone)

motor intruding, warning of his approach. The golf cart stopped about fifty yards away. I was trapped. We both knew this was silly and were clearly uncomfortable. I had wandered in on some random path, and asked if this was really Mr. Cooksey's property, too. I even asked if I could plead my case to Mr. Cooksey himself, and was surprised when the guard began dialing his number on his cell phone.

I tried to reason with Mr. Cooksey. In his good ol' boy southern drawl he told me he had no insurance to cover me if something happened, and had no choice but to ask me to leave. The guard smiled as if to say I told you so, but I could tell his victory did not feel entirely sweet. I packed my things and walked back out the way I had come in.

I went back again before the bulldozers came. I found another path, waited for the small window between when the developer had the deed in his hands and the actual construction began. I managed to capture some of what

Cooksey's Campground once was, here, in this book, so we might recall what one paradise looked like when it was our own backyard.

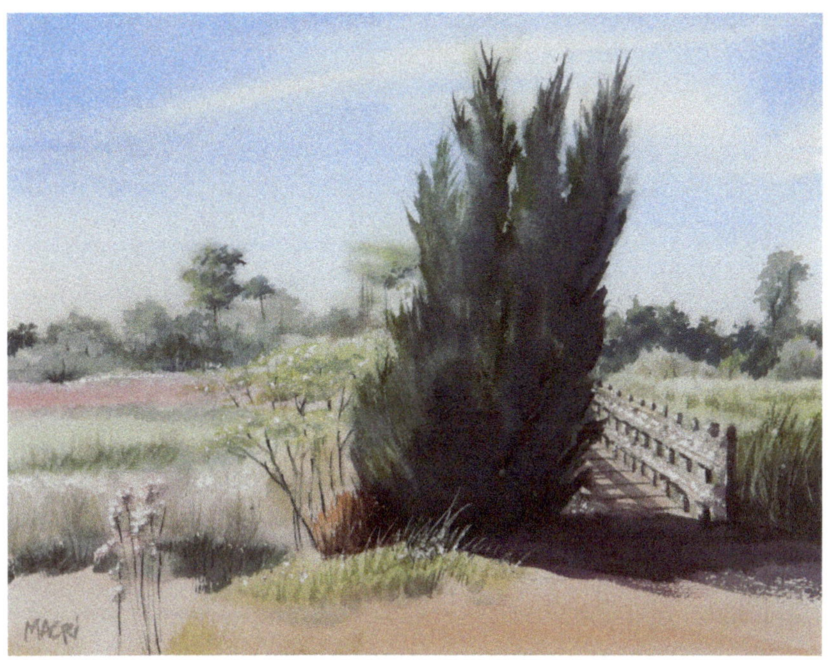

"Cedar next to Boardwalk"

Acknowledgements...

My sincere appreciation to all those who offered advice and helped me as I worked on this book:

The color photographs were taken by Walter Coker of Coker Photography with additional photography by Tom Brock of Archival Prints.

Aaron Bromirski took care of the graphic design, including front and back cover design and layout of all the pages in the book.

Leslie Cohen edited the text. (CohenCopyediting@gmail.com)

I appreciate all those who provided input and support for this book, especially Melissa Stuart, who has always championed my work and provided encouragement.

I want to thank the publisher, Legacies & Memories, and its president, E.L. (Ed) Wilks. He also offered suggestions on various aspects of the book's content, as well as marketing.

Without the help of many people, this book might never have been completed.

Thanks to anyone I have inadvertently forgotten to mention.

Nancy Macri

Contact Nancy Macri

E-mail: macrinancy@gmail.com

www.ingramcontent.com/pod-product-compliance
Lightning Source LLC
Chambersburg PA
CBHW050043040726
47599CB00015B/1782